D1569402

PUBLIC WORKS AND POVERTY ALLEVIATION IN RURAL CHINA

PUBLIC WORKS AND POVERTY ALLEVIATION IN RURAL CHINA

Zhu Ling and Jiang Zhongyi*

Nova Science Publishers, Inc.

New York

Art Director: Maria Ester Hawrys
Assistant Director: Elenor Kallberg
Graphics: Eddie Fung, Barbara Minerd, and Kerri Pfister
Manuscript Coordinator: Gloria H. Piza
Book Production: Gavin Aghamore, Joanne Bennette, Michele Jaeger
Christine Mathosian and Tammy Sauter
Circulation: Irene Kwartiroff and Annette Hellinger

Library of Congress Cataloging-in-Publication Data
available upon request

ISBN 1-56072-395-5

© 1996 by Nova Science Publishers, Inc.
6080 Jericho Turnpike, Suite 207
Commack, New York 11725
Tele. 516-499-3103   Fax 516-499-3146
E Mail Novascil@aol.com

All rights reserved. No part of this book may be reproduced, stored in a retrieval system or transmitted in any form or by any means: electronic, electrostatic, magnetic, tape, mechanical photocopying, recording or otherwise without permission from the publishers

Printed in the United States of America

Contents

Acknowledgments...iv

1

Introduction...1
Objective of the Study 1
Approach of the Research 4

2

**Anti-Poverty Strategies and
Yigong-Daizhen Policies of China**...........................7
Measurement of the Poor 7
Causes of the Poverty and Distribution of the Poor 12
Changes in the Anti-Poverty Strategies 16
Yigong-Daizhen Policies 22

3

Yigong-Daizhen Projects in Studied Regions...............27
Studied Provinces/Autonomous Region.......................27
Counties under the Survey 36
Organizational Patterns of Yigong-Daizhen Works...............51

4

Infrastructure of Sample Villages 57
Village Communities 57
Sample Villages 60
Roles of Village Communities in Construction of Public Works 71
Summary 82

5

Household and Individual Participants
of Yigong-Daizhen Projects 83
The Sample Population 83
Comparison between Participants and Nonparticipants 85
Selection of the Participants 96
Summary 100

6

Impact of the Projects on Property
and Income Distribution 103
Income Composition of Sample Households 103
Income Inequalities 110
Relation between Projects and Family Welfare 115
Determinants of Income 121
Property, Debt, and Investment of Sample Households 124
Conclusion and Its Policy Implication 130

7

Food Consumption and Nutrition
of Sample Households 133
Consumption Expenditures 134
Family Nutrition Status 136
Policy Implications of Research Results 145

8

Discussion of Research Results 147
Effects of Yigong-Daizhen Projects 147
Current Problems in Implementing Projects
and Tentative Solutions 153

9

**Macro-Economic Constraints
on Anti-Poverty Programs** 163
Food Security 164
Possibilities of Increase in Nonagricultural Employment 167
Rural Social Services 171
Macro-Economic Constraints on Poverty Eradication Schemes 179

10

Summary 185

Appendix 193

Bibliography 195

Subject Index 205

ACKNOWLEDGMENTS

W e are extremely indebted to Joachim von Braun for his valuable suggestions, comments, and editorial assistance. Special thanks are expressed to Lynette Aspillera, Yisehac Yohannes, Jay Willis, Zhang Ming, Li Yezuqin, Xie Changhao, Li Shi, and Kong Jingyuan for providing useful assistance. The authors are also very grateful for the kind cooperation of the institutions and authorities interviewed at the central government level and in Guizhou, Shandong, Ningxia, and Sichuan Provinces in China. Deep gratitude is extended to the village committees and farmers' households visited in the four provinces.

Zhu Ling
Jiang Zhongyi

✽✽✽✽✽✽✽✽✽✽✽✽✽✽
INTRODUCTION
✽✽✽✽✽✽✽✽✽✽✽✽✽✽

OBJECTIVE OF THE STUDY

Poverty alleviation is a common issue facing the majority of the Third World countries. Since the 1970s, the fact that the number of the poor in some developing countries has increased together with the fact that economic growth has aroused widespread concern of the international community. Therefore, development economics stressed the trade-off between "efficiency" and "equity" under special circumstances and clearly differentiated the concept of "growth" from "development." From then on, how to alleviate and eliminate poverty while pursuing economic growth became a development issue.

The poverty studies from the perspective of socioeconomic development focuses on long-standing poverty inflicting some groups of people rather than short-term or individual cases of poverty caused by emergencies such as natural and man-made calamities. To be specific, poor population in accordance with the definition given by developing countries refers to those groups of people in absolute poverty. Long-standing poverty can be classified into two categories by the origins of the poverty: (1) class-based poverty owing to great disparity in distribution of property ownership; and (2) regional poverty resulting from adverse living environment (lack of resources and underdeveloped infrastructure). Of course, some cases of poverty can be attributable to the simultaneous effect of the above two factors.

At present, poverty in China is manifested as regional poverty in the rural society. Unlike the countries which allow free migration of population, the poor of China are concentrated in rural areas. The adoption of the household residential registration system since the 1950s set up barriers between urban and rural societies. Urban inhabitants enjoy stable social welfare to satisfy their basic necessities such as clothing, food, shelter, and transportation. The welfare system is not yet to cover rural population. In addition to this, unlike countries with private land ownership, the land reform and the collective land tenure system initiated more than four decades ago uprooted once and for all class-based poverty from unequal distribution of land ownership. However, the regional poverty left over from history continued to the present day. Before economic reform, this type of poverty blended with widespread poverty of the rural population and did not appear noticeable. Though it was not until the mid-1980s that the Chinese government expressly raised the issue of poverty, poor population was by no means a product of rapid economic growth at that period. The living conditions of the poor did not worsen with economic growth and reform in the individual income distribution system. The case was the extent of their improvement was below the national average.

Market-oriented economic reforms at the end of the 1970s endowed farmers with autonomy in operation. Most of them exploited the chances of raised prices for farm products, structure adjustment, and development of nonfarming industries, and allocated their resources in a more efficient way. As a result, their household income grew by a wide pace in a short span of several years. In comparison, about one tenth of rural population only received very limited benefits from the changes, without even solving their problems of food security. The areas they inhabit either lack both resources and infrastructure or enjoy resource potentials with poor infrastructure. The common phenomenon is the widening gap between these areas and the national average in socioeconomic development. Precisely owing to this, the Chinese government began to launch a massive antipoverty campaign in

1985, with priority given to accelerating development of poverty-stricken areas and ensuring the basic needs of poor population for food and clothing.

Obviously, compared with those of South-East Asian, African, and Latin American countries, China's poverty alleviation undertaking is at an initial stage. These countries have accumulated rich experiences over the past two decades' practice and summed up many theories on poverty alleviation by international and domestic scholars. China's explorations in the progress of economic reforms have but features in institutional innovation and achieved remarkable results in only a few years. In-depth and careful research on specific subjects and theoretical summary of experiences during this period of time will not only be used as references for China's future efforts in poverty alleviation, but will also be helpful to other developing countries.

"To offer job opportunities to replace sheer relieves" (Yigong-daizhen in Chinese) is one of the poverty alleviation policies. The major content of the policy is that government carries out investment in kind in infrastructure construction of the poor areas, which, on one hand, creates a basis for local economic growth, and, on the other hand, provides short-term employment and income for poor population. This is what the international community terms as public works. This study focuses on the examination of the role of "Yigong-daizhen" projects in poverty alleviation. First, the study defines the extent of direct benefits the poor reap by referring to income and social services acquired by the farmers involved in the projects. Second, the study analyzes the employment, property, income structures, and nutrition status of the beneficiaries of the projects and determines the indirect social benefits. Third, the study notes the limitations of "Yigong-daizhen" projects from the perspective of poverty alleviation and identifies the existing problems of project organizations and ways of operation and measures for improvement. Building upon these, the study will predict the influence of further introduction of market mechanisms on "Yigong-daizhen" projects and living conditions of poor population, and looks into the possibility of participation of the poor and their benefitting from overall national economic growth and development under new circumstances.

APPROACH OF THE RESEARCH

"Yigong-daizhen" projects emphasize construction of roads and drinking water supply systems. The former aims at improving transportation for the poor, while the latter intends to provide them with a kind of social service. In order to find out the effects of the project implementation, the author paid visits to the State Planning Commission, the Leading Group on Economic Development of Poor Areas under the State Council, Ministry of Transportation, Ministry of Water Conservancy, and other competent authorities in 1990 to collect information on project planning, investment regulations, materials appropriation, project organization, and implementation. Moreover, case studies on road construction in Guizhou and drinking water supply project in Sichuan (Ling 1990) were conducted. Yet, this research is only at the macro level.

With a view to further inquiring the impact of the projects on the poor, research at the micro level was conducted in 1992. In May and June of the same year, a sample survey was made in three counties, including 34 villages and 360 peasant households. Before this, a pre-test was carried out in Laiyuan County, Hebei Province, in 1991. Based on this, the design of a sample survey and questionnaire were revised. The finalized sample program is described as follows:

1. Three poor counties are selected, respectively, from developed, average-developed, and less-developed provinces, namely Linqu County from Shandong, Wangcang County from Sichuan, and Xiji County from Ningxia, in order to observe the impact of the projects on different types of the poor areas.

2. Case studies and pre-tests indicate households in the same village in a poor area have similar economic activities and incomes, while households in different villages have strikingly different conditions. Besides, moving earth and stone for the construction work in the project is normally completed by a village as the basic unit, the survey at village community level becomes highly significant for the entire research. Therefore, the number of sample villages from each county is

increased to the level worthwhile for group division and the number of sample households from each village is reduced correspondingly. Finally, 12 administrative villages are chosen from each county with four villages forming a group. The first group represents villages taking part in a road building project. The second group are villages engaged in completing a drinking water supply project. The third group serves as reference villages which are not yet to be involved in any "Yigong-daizhen" projects. Village questionnaires are filled in by talking with major members of the Village Committee.

3. A household questionnaire was designed for interviewing the 10 households picked at a random sample from each village, which will help collect data in 1991.

It is worth mentioning that the choice of studied provinces made reference to suggestions from the State Planning Commission, Ministry of Transportation, and Ministry of Water Conservancy; surveyed counties were recommended by authorities in charge of "Yigong-daizhen" from Shandong, Ningxia, and Sichuan Provinces, respectively; the determination of sample villages resulted from discussions with project management institutions of the three counties. Because of poor transportation, only two villages from Wangcang of Sichuan Province were selected as reference group, with 20 sample households of each of the two. So the total number of sample households from three counties remained unchanged; the figure was 360, of which 358 filled-out household questionnaires were valid ones.

In order to ensure the quality of data collection, enumerators were trained, pending their households interviews. Indices of the questionnaires were explained one by one and methods of inquiries were expounded with great emphasis on inviting the housewife of each sample household in the interview. Originally the accountant of each sample village was expected to work as an enumerator. Yet, transportation and the education background of the population in the three counties are quite different. The following adjustments had to be made: in Xiji County, the rural survey team of the County Statistic Bureau undertook the survey; in Wangcang, working staff from the County Water Conservancy Bureau and Transportation Bureau were chosen for the interviews in the villages and the households; only in Linqu were accountants from sample villages engaged in the survey as enumerators.

Data gathered from the sample survey were supplemented by Statistical Yearbook and information published by the State Statistic Bureau and materials provided by relevant functionary departments, such as the State Planning Commission, Ministry of Finance, Ministry of Transportation, Ministry of Water Conservancy, Statistic Yearbooks of the studied provinces and counties, working reports on "Yigong-daizhen" and historical documents in the fields of culture, geography, and economy of the three counties.

Based on processing and statistic analysis of the abovementioned documents and data, Chapters 2 and 3 give a brief overview of antipoverty strategies and "Yigong-daizhen" policies in China in the 1980s and elaborate on the demand on "Yigong-daizhen" by virtue of major socioeconomic indices from the areas under the survey. In Chapters 4 and 5, comparisons between social service facilities of different sample villages and income levels of different sample households will help identify the characteristics of the beneficiaries of the projects. Chapters 6 to 8 are devoted to analyzing properties and incomes, diversified activities, and nonfarming employment as well as the nutrition status of the sample households from benefitted villages and non-benefitted ones. Furthermore, the social benefits of "Yigong-daizhen" projects will also be discussed. Chapter 9 employs development theories to interpret the analysis results of the previous chapters and make evaluation on policies and projects of "Yigong-daizhen." Existing problems will be pointed out and impact of the marketization of the national economy on the poor will be forecasted. Chapter 10 sums up the research and lists conclusions.

ANTI-POVERTY STRATEGIES AND "YIGONG-DAIZHEN" POLICIES OF CHINA

W ith regional differences in socioeconomic development and disparities in personal income distribution widened continuously in China during the economic reforms of the 1980s, the Chinese government expressly raises the issue of poverty alleviation and lists it as one of the important parts of socioeconomic development policies. Pending this, more attention was focused on uneven development at a provincial level and regional policies were employed to narrow the gap between "developed" and "underdeveloped" areas. The fact that the concept of "poverty" is now used publicly displays the importance the government attaches to the status of individual and household earnings in relation to economic growth. Therefore, the formulation of anti-poverty strategies is based on the identification of poor population and targeted at helping them emerge from poverty.

MEASUREMENT OF THE POOR

The definition and measurement of poverty is the primary question to be answered in working out a poverty alleviation policy. Up to now, the term "poverty" used in China, both theoretically and practically, has been in its economic sense, and especially in the sense of the absolute poverty. That is to say, it means "the individual or household whose earnings and other income cannot meet his or the household's basic needs of living" (Rural Survey Team of the State Statistical Bureau 1989). Such understandings were clearly reflected in the antipoverty strategies. The solution of clothing and food shortage problem, for example, enjoyed the priority in government targets for poverty alleviations. Standard for the identification of the poor was based on the estimated amount of food and the level of income necessary for the existence of an individual or a household. However, the low-income level and underdevelopment in social sector (living environment, illiteracy, death rate of infancy, life expectancy, and so forth) used to coincide with each other in the poor areas, so that the poor identified according to the lowest living standard in such areas were usually characterized by the two features.

Poverty line is the most frequently used indicator to identify the poor people, poor households, and poor areas, and on the basis of which to calculate the incidence of poverty (poor population/overall population). The poverty line used in Chinese poverty alleviation practices was fixed in 1984, based on the large-scale case studies taken by the Rural Development Research Center of the State Council. The studied areas then covered were mainly the border provinces and the inland mountainous and arid regions (Liaison Office of the Research Center for Rural Development under the State Council, 1984). Meanwhile, the natural resource investigation organized by the National Committee for Agricultural Divisions also provided a large amount of information for the calculation of poverty lines (Lei Xilu and Li Renbao 1980).

As farmers' households became basic units of production and living during the economic reforms, per capita foodgrain and per capita income of a household were taken as the measurement for poverty dimensions. The Rural Development Research Center of the State Council first set the poverty line at the standard of 120 yuan per capita income and 200 kilograms per capita foodgrain of a household. Provinces all over the country were requested to count up accordingly the number of their respective poor population and report to the higher level the poor counties. The data collected at the beginning of 1985 showed that there were altogether 14 million poor households in the country and a poor population of more than 70 million, representing approximately 9 percent of the total rural population (Ministry of Civil Affairs and others 1985).

Based on the information concerning poor households and areas, the central government then decided to make special appropriations for poverty alleviation purposes. Attracted by the financial support of the central government, a number of the provincial governments gave an account of more poor than what was before. Then, the poor in need of support reported by provinces at the 1985 Rural Working Conference numbered altogether 130 millions. Toward this, leading members of the central authorities pointed out that due to the limited financial resources, even though more poor counties and the poor were reported, it would not be possible to increase more appropriations. It was agreed upon that the central authorities would identify the poor counties which would enjoy the support of the nation. The problem faced then was how to narrow down the limits of the assistance. The Rural Development Research Center suggested that per capita foodgrain of 200 kilograms and per capita income of 200 yuan be taken as the poverty line. This was exactly the well-known standard of poverty line later on. Calculated on this standard, the national rural poor were 102 million people at the end of 1985, representing 12.2 percent of the rural total (Office of the Leading Group for Economic Development of Poor Areas under the State Council 1989a).

In 1986, the 4th session of the 6th National People's Congress included the poverty alleviation, as an important target, in the 7th Five-Year Plan of the national economic and social development, to support the poor areas extricating themselves from the economic and cultural backwardness as soon as possible. However, the 331 poor counties directly supported by the State during the 7th Five-Year Plan period were identified according to the following income level: per capita net income below 150 yuan in 1985, or per capita net income below 200 yuan in minority counties and the counties of the former revolutionary base areas. In certain special cases in the former revolutionary base areas, the standard for a poor county was fixed at per capita net income of below 300 yuan. Besides, 368 poor counties were identified by different provinces in the light of their local conditions and were to be supported by the respective provinces themselves (Office of the State Council Leading Group for Economic Development of Poor Regions 1991), among which were those having been reported at the end of 1985 but failed to be granted by the State.

It is thus evident that the poverty line was not the only standard to identify the poor to be supported. There were considerations of political stability as well as regional balance of interests. Even the finally fixed poverty line reflected the results of compromises between the central and the local governments. Of course, there would be no doubt that all the counties and people identified either by the State or by the provinces as the poor were of the poor stratum. The national average of the per capita net income of a rural household in 1985 was 398 yuan. Even the households with a 200 yuan per capita net income represented only the level of half the national average.

It should be noted here that with the performance of the poverty alleviation programs, the studies on poverty indices also developed. However, the poverty lines defined in the theoretical explorations were not the same as the standards used in the poverty alleviation practices. For example, the central government decided that during the 8th Five-Year Plan period, an additional annual credit of 500 million yuan would be used specially for the poverty alleviation purposes, so as to speed up the economic development of the counties with a per capita net income of farmers' households below 300 yuan. Does it mean then the heightening of poverty line and the increase of the poor population in China? The answer is "no." It only showed that the government had determined to increase the input in the poor areas. With a purpose to effectively use this newly increased credit, 214 additional poor counties were identified by the State Council Leading Group for Poverty Alleviation, while the original poor counties supported by the State during the 7th Five-Year Plan period would enjoy continuously the same assistance it received previously. The newly increased poor counties had originally been within the range of the poor areas. They failed to be identified as poor counties during the 7th Five-Year Plan period either because of the limitations of the financial ability of the central government, or because of the fact that their respective per capita net income in 1985 was higher than the standard of identification for the poor, while in other years they were below the poverty lines.

What is actually the level of income indicated by the poverty line, based on the definition of absolute poverty? What is exactly the poor population thus estimated? To answer these questions, on the basis of data concerning family livelihood from nearly 67,000 rural sample households, comparing per capita net income with basic living expenses and taking into account the standard of essential nutrition (per capita daily intake of 2,400 calories) as well as the lowest requirements for other necessary consumptions, the General Team for Rural Survey of the State Statistical Bureau (SSB) defined the poverty line in 1988 as per capita net income of 260 yuan and estimated national rural poor population at 120 million, with 28.04 million poor households and 250 poverty-stricken counties. Accordingly, the calculations showed that the rural poverty rate was 13.9 percent, the rate of poor households was 13.4 percent, and the rate of poor counties was 10.6 percent. Besides, the status of the poor in 1988 was also indicated in the research by the extent of the income gap rate of the rural poor population calculated through the formula:

$$\frac{\text{poverty line - per capita net income of the poor}}{\text{poverty line}}$$

The result showed that it was 22 percent.

According to such calculations, does it mean that the poor population in 1988 was 18 million more than that in 1985 (120 million - 102 million)? For this, it is necessary to clarify that the number of rural poor in 1985 was calculated on the basis of the data reported by different provinces, while the statistics for 1988 were calculated based on the sample surveys. With sources and methods being different, the differences in the results should not be deemed as strange. In the author's opinion, the report drafted by the General Team for Rural Survey should be regarded as containing authoritative statistics on poor population in view of the reliability of data from SSB.

CAUSES OF THE POVERTY AND
DISTRIBUTION OF THE POOR

As known to all, western provinces fall into the category of underdeveloped areas when comparing the socioeconomic development indices of provinces in mainland of China. The existing gaps in development in the east, west, and inland of Chinese mainland were taking shape early in the history. The concept of Western China used by most scholars comprised the 11 provinces and autonomous regions of Yunnan, Guizhou, Sichuan, and Xizang (Tibet) in the southwest; Shaanxi, Gansu, Ningxia, Qinghai, and Xinjiang in the northwest; Inner Mongolia in the north; and Guangxi in the middle south. Some people thought that the concept of western China represented only the geographical position of the area, so that Inner Mongolia should not be included in it (Shi Zheng 1985). The concept of western China used by the State Planning Commission in the 7th Five-Year Plan included only nine provinces and autonomous regions exclusive of Inner Mongolia and Guangxi. It is necessary to make it clear that the idea of western China used in the following discussions of this study would be the concept of the 11 provinces and autonomous regions unless those with specific explanations.

For most of the western provinces and autonomous regions, poor in agricultural resource has been the common roots of poverty in the rural areas. The Chinese topography of being high in the west and low in the east has caused 76 percent of the counties in the 11 western provinces and autonomous regions to be identified as mountainous, semi-mountainous, or hilly counties. Except for the plateau of Yunnan and Guizhou, all the western regions are climatically dry, with annual rainfalls in Inner Mongolia and the five northwest provinces below 400 millimeters. In Guizhou, Yunnan, and Guangxi, where there is more rainfall, 60 percent of the counties are situated in the areas with karst topography. It is obvious that such natural conditions are not in favor of the development of crop production.

With the low output of the land, forests were continuously felled by the local people to expand the area under cultivations. However, with the low productivity of the land, such efforts of reclamations had only encouraged the increase of the population. The natural growth rate of the population in the western provinces had always been higher than the national average, ever since 1965. During the period from 1965 to 1985, the national population growth rate reduced from 2.84 percent to 1.12 percent, while the rate in the 11 western provinces reduced from 3.96 percent to 1.44 percent. Especially in the provinces of Ningxia, Qinghai, and Guangxi, their respective population growth rate topped, in turn, all the other provinces of the nation (Institute of Population Research 1987). The fast population growth had partly been caused by the preferential policies for family planning of minority nationalities who concentratedly live in the western regions. Besides, it was also because of the fact that the inhabitants there were so scattered in mountainous areas that it was difficult for the implementation of various family planning measures. Thus, the interaction of population growth and the large-scale damage of forests in the course of land reclamation wrecked the ecological environment. The rate of forest cover in the western regions in 1985 was 7.5 percent (0.3 to 3.9 percent in the provinces of Gansu, Ningxia, Qinghai, and Xinjing). The area of soil erosion in the same year was 67 million hectares, representing 51.8 percent of the national total. The worsening ecological environment and the frequent natural calamities caused widespread shortages in food supply in those provinces.

The bad natural conditions, poor transportation facilities, and being ill-informed hindered the development of human resources. The education in the vast rural area of western China has long been in a state of backwardness, with the rural illiteracy rate above 12 years of age being as high as 50 percent, which is one-third higher than the national average and a situation capable of being described as the "poverty in knowledge." Due to the bad nutrition and sanitary conditions, the average life expectancy of the rural population in the western regions has been shorter than the national average. In 1981, for example, the average life expectancy in the nine provinces of the southwest and the northwest was 58 to 65 years old, 2 to 9 years shorter than the national average (Institute of Population Research 1988).

The various disadvantages discussed above not only caused the backwardness in the commodity production of the western regions but also seriously hampered the enterprising spirit of the people there. As a result, a sense of lacking self-confidence and being apathetic to existing conditions has been growing among the rural poor. Even in areas with favorable natural conditions, the area Xishuangbanna of Yunnan Province, for instance, there exist poor in general. Such a phenomenon was summarized as "the poverty of plenty" (Wang Xiaoqiang and Bai Nanfeng 1987).

In the mountainous regions of central and eastern China, there are also poor people inhabited, and problems similar to those in the mountainous and the drought areas of the west. Hence, the formation of the concept of the "poor regions" which was, for the first time, contained in the documents of the leadership at the top level in the year of 1984 (circula of the Chinese Communist Party Central Committee and the State Council on Supporting Poor Regions to Alleviate Poverty As Soon As Possible, September of 1984). The concept "poor regions" used here was not the equivalent of the "western regions," notwithstanding the fact that the poor in the western regions was 80 percent of the national total. The "poor regions" here actually represented the 18 belts all over the country where large amounts of poor people were concentrated, such as the Wumeng Mountain Region, the Taihang Mountain Region, the Drought area of Dingxi of Gansu Province, and so forth. Considered from the angle of administrative divisions, the difference between the two concepts was the fact that the western regions were composed of provinces while the basic units of poor regions were counties.

Of the poor population, ethnic minorities normally live in ever more adverse surroundings, due to the fact that they were expelled to peripheral areas unfavorable to agricultural production in history. Ever since the establishment of the People's Republic of China, it has annihilated the class inequality as well as the national discriminations. On this basis the central government has taken a series of policies to promote the social and economic development of the minority nationalities. But in certain areas inhabited by minority nationalities, the backwardness inherited from history has not yet been fundamentally removed. Of the 331 poor counties being specially supported by the state, 42.6 percent are minority counties. Up to the end of 1988, there was still a population of 13 to 14 million people whose food and clothing supply remaining insecure, representing 40 percent of total rural population of the overall minority poor counties. About 70 percent of this population living below the poverty line belonged to the minority nationalities (Li Changan 1991).

The factors from which the poor of the minority nationalities originated comprised of those same for the nonminority poor and those related to the special social and cultural backgrounds of the minorities. The collectivization in the 1950s did more to hurt the social and economic development of the areas inhabited by the minority nationalities than to the developed areas. It is because there had been small-size commodity production in those developed areas, so that as soon as the system of People's Commune was dissolved, the farmers were able to restore immediately their farms and engage in market-oriented activities. But in the areas where the minority nationalities inhabited, the system of the People's Communes was carried out immediately after the abolition of either the feudal system or the remaining system of slave-ownerships, or the even more ancient system of primitive communities, thus pushing the small-scale subsistence economies overnight into large-scale ones (Du Runsheng 1986). Therefore, laborers in the areas were not capable of running independently the commodity production after the abolition of the People's Communes. Moreover, living in isolated environment and inactive in accepting new ideas, the minority poor, having been accustomed to the life of "big pan meals," are not easy in changing their habit, too. Even more annoying are certain traditional customs and superstitious beliefs so far hindering the employment of modern tools in production and the spread of scientific and technical knowledge (Zhang Xietang 1988). All these factors widened the gaps between the minority regions and the national average in the social and economic development.

The basic living units of the poor are households. In some African and South American countries, the husband and wife of a household have separate accounts. In certain cases, the accounts were divided due to the separation of the land ownership with the output of the land also divided accordingly. In some other cases, the "spheres of influence" were "carved out" due to labor divisions, with women growing foodgrain and responsible for the foodgrain income and men engaging in the management of cash crops, thus controlling the cash income. Besides, the female-headed households were usually in an unfavorable economic situation. In such developing countries, social inequality between the male and female played a role in the formation of the poverty of women and children. The government-supported movement of women's liberation in China and the policy of equal pay for equal work between men and women have effectively helped the participation of Chinese women in the social and economic activities in an extent much higher than that in other developing countries. Even though the inequalities between men and women in China have not yet been completely wiped out, the tradition of pooling family incomes in the same money box has successfully kept the members of a same family at the same living standard and made it difficult to be divided into two strata of the ordinary poor and the abject poverty. In addition, even if women-headed households are poorer than average families, this has normally not resulted from discrimination against women. More often than not, it is attributable to lack of young and strong manpower in this type of households.

CHANGES IN THE ANTI-POVERTY STRATEGIES

In essence, poverty alleviation activities in China represent government actions. The recipient units identified by the central and provincial governments are poor counties. The county governments transfer assistance to poor households by virtue of financial or administrative organizations at township and village level. This form of arrangement enables poverty alleviation strategies pursued by the Chinese government to be characterized by two features distinct from other developing countries. First, they are directly targeted at regions instead of individual rural households. Second, nongovernmental organizations and the poor have very limited participation in the decision making process. Therefore, a series of policy reforms related to socioeconomic development of poverty-stricken areas marks the turning point in poverty alleviation strategies in the 1980s.

The peculiarities in the running of economy in poor areas before the reforms were once described as the "blood-drawing operation" (Guo Fansheng 1988) and the "blood transfusion mechanism." What was indicated by the first description was the fact that under the system of planned economy, the raw materials of the poor areas could only be transferred by low prices to the developed areas for processing, while the second description referred to the phenomenon that the funds accumulated in the developed areas were allocated by the Central Government to the poor areas as financial subsidies or public investments, which not only failed to become a potentiality in the development of the local economy but encouraged the tendency of dependence of the local government and the poor people.

So, starting from 1985, the Central Government pursued an antipoverty policy with a lot of emphases on helping poverty-ridden areas set up "blood forming mechanism" (Office of the Leading Group for Economic Development of Poor Areas under the State Council 1989b):

1. To replace the old poverty alleviation method of merely providing reliefs by the new way of making policy alterations in the field of production so as to bring into full play the initiatives of the cadres and masses to promote the development of commodity economy and mobilize the inherent economic vitalities of the poor areas.

2. To make a change-over from the old way of sharing out the funds equally in the implementation of the poverty alleviation measures to a new practice of alleviating poverty in one poor area after another and in different batches through concentrated use of manpower, funds, and materials. As for those dispersedly located poor townships, villages, and households in nonpoor regions, it would be the duty of the local county government to design and finance poverty alleviation programs for them.

3. To give more decision making power to farmers and herdsmen of the poor areas in running economy, for example, the freedom to sell farming, forestry, animal husbandry, and subsidiary and local special products, except those belonging to the reserved medical resources.

4. Reduction or remission of taxation.

5. To build up rural roads, jointly invested by the central and the local governments as well as the inhabitants of the poor areas themselves, in order to improve local infrastructure.

6. To promote comprehensive investment in the poor areas in the fields
of science and technology, education, health care, forestry, water
conservancy projects, and so forth, organized by functional ministries
concerned at the central level.

The measures listed above were obviously aiming at, on the one hand,
helping the governments and people of the poor areas to develop their
economies by self-reliance, and, on the other hand, making trials of raising
the efficiency of the utilization of poverty alleviation funds. This can be
considered the introduction of an efficiency-oriented poverty alleviation
strategy.

Under the guidance of this strategy, the ways of allocating and employ-
ing resources for poverty alleviation also undertook major changes. First of
all, a major part of funds could no longer be used free of charge. Of 4.55
billion yuan of poverty alleviation funds appropriated by the Central Government each year, around 78 percent were loans granted by banks in inter-
est-subsidized forms. The rest were direct appropriations from the Ministry
of Finance without repayments obligation. Besides, functionary departments
of the Central Government allocated poverty alleviation funds on specialized
projects to underdeveloped provinces on a sectorial basis, in accordance
with their respective poverty alleviation programs, which belonged to unpaid
utilization of resources.

Second, the appropriation of poverty alleviation funds on the basis of
projects aimed at building up productive capacity in the localities and promoting economic growth. Among all investment projects, infrastructure construction mainly made use of nonrepayment funds and took public investment as a form of implementation. "Yigong-daizhen" (a Chinese term
meaning "to provide works instead of reliefs") projects belonged to this
category. Direct production projects were mostly financed by loans. Of
these, industrial enterprises set up by agent organizations of county and
township governments occupied an overriding share of investment.

The rapid growth of the rural economy in nonpoor regions in the early
1980s helped most of the rural population to extricate themselves from the
state of poverty. So, the economic growth was then regarded as the funda-

mental access towards the alleviation of the regional poverties. The distribution pattern of investment displayed exactly the pursuit of growth. A State Council Circula (issued in October of 1987, on "strengthening the economic development in poor regions"), while stressing that the work of poverty alleviations should be done down to the households, also pointed out that it did not mean simply to share out the poverty alleviation funds among the households, but to initiate economic entities, that is, the enterprises, for poverty alleviation purposes. It is exactly these enterprises which should provide opportunities of employment for the labor of the poor households and bring along large numbers of households to engage in the development of commodity productions. In other words, it means to establish new growth points with the enterprises as a core. The expansion of enterprises promotes the economic growth, on the one hand, and, on the other, conducts the increased incomes into the hands of a considerable part of the poor. Hence, nearly 80 percent of the poverty alleviation loans went to the enterprises during the period of 1986-1990, with the remaining part of the total being invested in the households for the development of planting, breeding, and other diversified agricultural activities (Zhou Binbin 1990).

The problem lies in the fact that poverty alleviation strategy of economic growth won success only in certain poor areas with resource potentials (for example, mineral deposits or mountain forests), better natural conditions, and not the worst transportation facilities. In regions with poor resource, bad environment, and difficult transportation, there were more failures than success in the investments made in enterprises, which were either in a state of depression or had gone bankrupt, holding, in vain, huge amounts of poverty alleviation funds, only to the disadvantage of the majority of the poor who had lost their opportunity of getting the funds to develop their own business.

The efficiency-oriented strategy and the strategy of regional economic growth had effectively helped the nonhard-core poor across the poverty threshold, but it was also found that, under the strategies, the poverty alleviation funds were difficult to reach the hands of those hard-core poor. Even more difficult was the solution of their problem of foodgrain shortages. It was because, first, most of the poverty alleviation funds were granted as

credit which needed the ability of paying back and a position to find necessary mortgages, both of which were headaches to the hard-core poor. Second, it was also because of the fact that to increase the per unit area yield of
foodgrain in poor areas needed long-term investments with a lower return
rate, while the banks, when granting credit, tended to give priority to those
projects with smaller investments and quick repayment so as to avoid risk.
Besides, it would be even higher costs and even bigger risks if only to rely
on the purchase of foodgrain to meet the requirements of the poor, because
the government, at the moment, could hardly bear the burden of paying subsidies for transportation expenses and the poor could also not afford to pay
higher purchasing prices.

It was obvious that the targets of regional economic growth and the targets of the poverty alleviation did not necessarily coincide each other completely. The decisionmakers pointed out that in the 1990s, the poverty alleviation campaign must be extended to those areas in the deep mountains,
rocky mountains, and high mountains, to those poorest, most backward, and
in the most remote and isolated areas, in particular to those areas inhabited
by minority nationalities. Thus, the food security in these hard-core poor
areas was listed as the first important issue to be solved (Chen Junsheng
1991). An important measure taken in this direction was to invest the yearly
one million tons of foodgrain, allotted by the State Planning Commission
specially for the programs of public works, in the fundamental farmland
construction projects in an effort to realize the target of one mu fundamental
farmland for every person set in the 8th Five-Year Plan for economic and
social development. Here the term "fundamental farmland" ("Ji Ben Nong
Tian" in Chinese) means the farmland capable of ensuring stable and high
yields despite drought or excessive rain. This policy itself was described as
the policy of "to get more foodgrain with foodgrain."

Besides stressing food security for the poor, poverty alleviation strategies
in the 1990s may be expected to attach more importance to improvement of
social services. The discussion of people-centered development strategies in
the international community has had a positive impact on the study and formulation of poverty alleviation strategies in China. Domestic policy researchers have been making unremitting efforts in clarifying the concept of

"development." For instance, a new development strategy was designed by the researchers of the Office of State Council Leading Group for Poverty alleviation, which called for the participation of all the rural poor in a program for the readjustment of the relations between man and resources, including the improvement of social services and ecological environment, the promotion of family planing, the polarization of primary education, the extension of appropriate technologies, carrying out capital construction of farmland and water conservation, the implementation of employment plans, and others (Zhou Binbin 1990). It was, in essence, a comprehensive strategy of social and economic development differentiating itself from the economic growth strategy by its special attention given to the development of human resources and the improvement of living qualities while stressing, as well, the increase in incomes of the poor. Obviously, it takes time to see the fruits of this type of reform. Yet its advancement has already marked a considerable progress in theoretical research and practice of poverty alleviation in China.

Here an additional point must be made to the above statements on the strategic changes: the existing anti-poverty measures have by no means been given up in the policy reform. The changes imply a turning of policy focuses and adoption of more approaches. For instance, although a specific institution in charge of poverty alleviation programs was set up, the system of the Ministry of Civil Affairs has continuously undertaken the function of sending relief to the poor; the investment in farmland capital construction was newly increased while the loans with subsidized interest have been further issued to the enterprises and farmers in the poor areas, and so forth.

The special support given to the poor regions and poor population reflected the intention of the Chinese government to attend to the problem of equality while pursuing the improvement of efficiencies along the courses of social and economic development. The reform in antipoverty policies since 1986 not only brought an increase in the comprehensive investment of funds, materials, technologies, and qualified human resources to the poor regions, but also established the efficiency-oriented system for poverty alleviation, thus enabling the regional poverties to be eased up gradually. Putting the per capita rural income of 350 yuan as the standard for the poor counties getting out of the "poverty threshold," then the share of such counties in the overall poor counties receiving key State aid was 31.4 percent in 1989. But regional differences still showed themselves up during the process of poverty alleviation. The share of poor counties having been extricated from poverty was 79 percent in the eastern regions, 35 percent in central China, and only 18 percent in the west in the same year (Rural Survey Team of the State Statistical Bureau 1990). Obviously, it is a far cry from the objective of poverty elimination. Especially under the circumstances of an unsound legal system, a lack of means in income redistribution, a weak social security system, and imperfect rules of market regulation, the quick transformation in 1992 of the national economy to a market system may bring about poverty based on unequal distribution of property. Then, China will be faced with a danger of growing a poor population.

YIGONG-DAIZHEN POLICIES

The end of 1984 witnessed the beginning of large-scale infrastructure construction in poor areas in the form of "Yigong-daizhen." This type of public investment differentiated from formal capital construction projects of the state in the following ways:

1. "Yigong-daizhen" projects were specially designed for assisting poor areas with rural poor population as direct beneficiaries. During the 1960s and 1970s, though there were road and bridge building, introduction of electricity, and diversion works in some poor mountainous areas, they served some military and industrial enterprises only. The infrastructure and enterprises as well belonged to urban society. Neither did they absorb local labor, nor help form a driving force to promote socioeconomic development of the poor areas. They were likened to isolated islands in a spacious sea, for they were detached from the social and economic lives of the rural areas.

2. The investment of the Central Government took the form of investment in kind (Table 2.1). These goods actually were surplus products during a certain period under the planned economy. Investment in kind in 1985-87 employed 2.7 billion yuan worth of stock grain, cotton, and cloth. Goods transferred in 1989-91 were medium- or low-grade overstocked industrial products with a value of 600 million yuan. When the urban consumption market was sluggish in 1990-92, an additional 1.5 billion yuan worth of industrial products were put in "Yigong-daizhen" projects. "Yigong-daizhen" projects during the first two periods were focused on building roads in townships and villages, and facilities of drinking water for people and animals. Investment planning in 1990-92 emphasized small-scale water conservation and capital construction of agricultural farmland (Regional Division under the State Planning Commission and the Sichuan Provincial Office for Yigong-daizhen 1991). In addition, a bulk of foodgrain, edible oil, and industrial goods valued at 2.5 billion yuan were allocated for farmland capital construction, harnessing big rivers, and construction of rural infrastructure in the period of 1991-97.

Table 2.1—Chinese government investment in Yigong-daizhen schemes, 1984-1993

Scheme Number	Period	Planned In-Kind Goods Invested	Converted Value of the Goods (billion yuan[a])	Project Focus
1	1984-87	Cereals, cotton, and cloth	2.7	Roads and drinking water supply facilities
2	1989-91	Medium- and low-grade consumer goods	0.6	Roads and drinking water supply facilities
3	1990-92	Industrial goods	1.5	Roads and drinking water supply facilities, farmland improvement
4	1991-95	Foodgrains	5.0	Terraced fields, small-scale water conservation
5	1991-95	Foodgrains and industrial goods	10.0	Big rivers
6	1993-97	Cereals, cloth, edible oil, medium- and low-grade consumer goods	10.0	Infrastructure, including clinics, health care stations for women and children

Source: Documents issued by the State Planning Commission referring to Yigong-daizhen schemes, 1984-1993.
[a]   In 1993, 5.8 yuan equaled US$1.

In line with relevant stipulations, goods allocated by the Central Government should be distributed to people involved in construction projects as wages. Local governments were supposed to raise supplementary funds at a ratio no lower than 1:1 to pay for project materials and other expenses. Yet in real practice, except for a few provinces which enjoyed powerful economic strength, most of the provinces and counties could not channel sufficient supplementary funds. As a result, poverty alleviation funds from other channels (such as functionary departments) were used to fill in the gap; on the other hand, part of the transferred goods were converted into money or consumer goods directly turned into input goods. This mobilized farmers to provide part of their labor free of charge and reduced wages for paid labor.

These practices are not workable in the implementation of general capital construction projects. Because of the striking poverty alleviation nature of "Yigong-daizhen" programs, local governments and the poor people accepted the practices and voluntarily participated in investment projects. The above flexible methods in contravention with stipulations became normal practices. At least, it played the positive role of pooling resources to improve infrastructure. There is no denying the fact that employment of unpaid labor with no restraints will undoubtedly reduce the present level of income of the poor by a wide margin. Public words aimed at poverty alleviation may make the poor even poorer in the short term.

3. "Yigong-daizhen" projects mainly made use of simple labor-intensive technology, so that local labor force became qualified workers. Large amounts of surplus labor were utilized. Normally, construction was carried out in slack seasons, which provided farmers with their sources of income to varying degrees.

From 1985 to 1991, the adoption of "Yigong-daizhen" policies in poor areas helped build 131,000 kilometers of roads and 7,900 bridges, and dredged 2,400 kilometers of inland river channels. Some 1,500 townships and more than 10,000 administrative villages have access to transport service and the problem of drinking water supply for 20 million people and 13 million animals has been resolved (Table 2.2). Thanks to these projects, not only transport facilities and social services of the poor areas have enjoyed effective improvement, but the quality of human resources in the localities has also experienced an upgrade. As a result, farmers mastered technical skills, administrative cadres learnt construction organization and management, and a contingent of specialized technical force has been trained in fields of transportation and water conservation.

Table 2.2—Major achievements of the Yigong-daizhen projects, China, 1985-90

Achievement	
Public roads	131,000 kilometers
Bridges (number)	7,972
Dredged river navigation routes	2,400 kilometers
Public roads connecting...	1,500 townships
	10,000 administrative villages
Drinking water supply for...	20,970,000 people
	13,560,000 animals

Source: Data from the State Planning Commission, 1988 and 1992.

The manifestation of enormous social benefits from road construction and drinking water supply for people and animals precisely answers the question of popularity and support that "Yigong-daizhen" policies enjoy from the poor people and of growing interest on the part of local governments. This prompts the Central Government to increase goods used in "Yigong-daizhen" programs, while enlarging the scope of the implementation (for instance, harnessing big rivers). All these lead to the fading of poverty alleviation features and inclusion of more administrative and management departments in the programs. Therefore, the organization of projects become increasingly complex and project development experiences difficulties. Against this background, the research on the organization features, ways of operation, and social benefits of "Yigong-daizhen" projects has great significance in policy improvement.

3

YIGONG-DAIZHEN PROJECTS
IN STUDIED REGIONS

T his chapter intends to describe generally the features of the social and economic developments in the investigated provinces and counties and give a brief account of the organizational patterns of the Yigong-daizhen projects (public works) there. The descriptions are designed to facilitate the further discussions in following chapters on the effects of such works in poverty alleviation. The background information as such will also help to explain the differences between various sample households in different regions.

STUDIED PROVINCES / AUTONOMOUS REGION

SHANDONG PROVINCE

Of the three investigated regions of Shandong, Ningxia, and Sichuan, Shandong leapt to join the ranks of the developed provinces only in the years of economic reforms of the 1980s, when its superiority in resources and in water and land transportation facilities were able to be fully utilized to create a miracle of pushing the provincial economic growth from a rate of

Table 3.1—Main social and economic indices of investigated provinces
           (regions) in 1980 and 1990

Indices	Shandong 1980	Shandong 1990	Ningxia 1980	Ningxia 1990	Sichuan 1980	Sichuan 1990	The Whole Nation 1980	The Whole Nation 1990
Population (millions)	72.96	84.93	3.74	4.66	98.16	108.13	987.05	1,143.33
Area (thousand square kilometers)	156.7	156.7	51.8	51.8	570.0	570.0	9,600	9,600
Per capita gross social production (yuan)*	805.5	3,825.5	722.2	2,502.4	556.2	2,090.2	864.6	3,323.3
Per capita financial revenue (yuan)	65.9	128.5	54.6	133.8	35.3	110.8	...	...
Per capita financial expenditure (yuan)	41.2	145.8	153.9	310.7	34.1	132.0	...	...
Per capita net income of rural households (yuan)	194.3	644.7	178.1	534.2	187.9	505.2	191.3	629.8
Gross agricultural production/gross social production (percent)	44.4	19.9	23.7	21.2	33.2	28.2	22.5	20.2
Rural population/total population (percent)	90.5	81.4	81.9	76.1	87.8	85.1	80.6	73.6
Rural poverty incidence (percent)	...	6.8	...	18.9	...	11.2	...	11.4
Rate of adult illiteracy (percent)	(27.5)	16.9	(27.0)	22.1	(23.0)	16.2	(22.8)	15.9
Infant mortality of those below one year old (percent)	2.02	...	6.19	...	6.00	...	4.25	3.76[b]
Per capita life expectancy (years)	70	...	66	...	64	...	67	69[c]
Rural per capita per day energy intake (calories)	...	2,522[d]	...	2,402	...	2,335	2,509[e]	2,543[d]

Source: Yearbook of Chinese Statistics (1991); Yearbook of Shandong Statistics (1991); Statistics
          Bureau of Ningxia (1991); Statistics Bureau of Sichuan Province (1992); World Bank (1992b);
          Yearbook of Chinese Population Census (1990); Yearbook of Chinese Population (1988, 1991); Chen
          Chunming (1992); sample survey conducted by the Chinese Academy of Preventive Medicine Science,
          Research Institute of Nutrition in 1989, see Chen Junshi and others (1991).

[a] "Gross social production," also termed as "gross social products" on certain occasions, means the
    total production value of the five material production sectors of agriculture, industry, construction,
    transportation and communication, and commerce (including catering trade and goods supply).

[b] Data for 1987; infant mortalities of the three provinces are data for 1981.

[c] Data belong to 1985; the remaining data belong to 1981.

[d] Results of the sample survey in 1989.

[e] The national average situation in 1980 is the result of the 1982 survey of nutrition situation.

moderate development to the level of one percentage point higher than the national average. During the period of 1980-1990, Shandong Province registered an average yearly increase of 10.1 percent in GNP, 10.2 percent in national income, and 9.2 percent in local revenue. The provincial per capita GNP reached RMB 1,548 yuan in 1990, ranking 11th among all Chinese provinces, except Taiwan, instead of 16th as in 1980 (see Table 3.1).

The economic take-off of Shandong Province had benefitted, first of all, from the rural economic reforms. Being a land with solid farming traditions, the province's output of cotton, wheat, groundnuts, flue-cured tobacco, and aquatic products had long been among the first three top producers among all the Chinese provinces. The price reform of farm produces at the end of the 1970s benefitted further the farmers of Shandong Province, from the big price increases with their personal income going up speedily and capital necessary for the development of rural nonfarming industries accumulated. The total output of rural enterprises in Shandong Province during the 10 years of 1980s increased 30 percent annually, on average, while absorbing a rural labor force as big as 9.44 million people. By the year 1990, the total output of township industries of Shandong had made up 42 percent of the overall industrial production of the province and farmers employed by the township enterprises or having a job outside their home villages amounted to 31 percent of the total rural labor force of the province (Shandong Provincial Statistical Bureau 1991).

Large-scale investments in basic industries and infrastructure have injected new energies for the rapid economic growth of Shandong Province. Situated in the east of the North China Plain, Shandong faces Japan and Korea across the sea to the east, adjoins the Chinese hinterland of Central plain to the west and enjoys a transportation network consisting of railways, public ways, and river and marine navigation ever since before the economic reforms. All these, in addition to its rich and diversified mineral reserves and aquatic resources, have rendered the province superior in attracting capital investments. During the past 10 years and more, the Chinese Central Government invested around 1,600 million yuan of RMB every year in the province, constituting more than 55 percent of the yearly total investment of

Table 3.2—Situation in studied counties in 1980 and 1990

Indices	Linqu 1980	Linqu 1990	Xiji 1980	Xiji 1990	Wangcang 1980	Wangcang 1990	Whole Nation 1980	Whole Nation 1990
Rural population (thousand)	703	826	284	361	340	352	810,960	895,903
Total rural households (thousands)	165	216	53.2[a]	65.4	75.3	103.8	173,470	222,372
Rural per capita farmland (mu)	1.3	0.9	6.8	3.0	0.9	0.8	1.7	1.7
Irrigated area/cultivated area (percent)	49.2	53.0	3.8	7.6	9.4	26.6	46.9	49.5
Multiple crop index (percent)	161.8	163.9	90.6	99.3	148.1	184.8	153.0	155.1
Chemical fertilizers applied per mu (kilogram)[b]	17.8	27.4	0.1	3.0	8.8	15.0	8.8	18.0
Foodgrain production per mu (kilogram)[c]	305.9	390.9	45.3	80.2	315.8	521.6	280.0	406.1
Gross agricultural production/gross rural social production (percent)[d]	...	41.7	...	79.3	...	64.2	68.9	46.1
Agricultural labor/rural labor (percent)	...	74.9	...	95.7	...	80.2	...	79.4
Road density (kilometer/hundred square kilometers)[e]	19.1	30.2	12.9	17.3	35.1	41.5	9.2	10.7
Population short of water (thousand people)[f]	211.5	99.2	319	213	187	74.3	120,000	31,000
Natural growth rate of population (percent)	0.96	1.08	2.04	2.94	-0.01	0.77	1.19	1.44
Rate of illiteracy (percent)	24.0	19.3	(44.0)[g]	37.0	...	(26.1)[g]	23.5	22.3
Infant mortality below one-year-old (percent)[h]	...	1.2	...	7.7	...	2.4	...	(5.9)
Per capita net income of rural households (yuan)	106.3	565	55	212	90.4	558	191.3	629.8

Source: State Statistical Bureau (1982, 1991); Linqu County History Editorial Board (1991); Xiji
          County Statistics Bureau (1984, 1990); Statistics Bureau of Wangcang County (1981, 1990);
          State Statistics Bureau, Department of Social Statistics of Chinese Countryside (1989);
          State Statistics Bureau, General Team for Social Economy in Chinese Countryside (1992);
          Ministry of Water Conservancy and Irrigation (1980); Office of the State Council Poverty
          Alleviation Leading Group (1991).

[a] Data of 1984.
[b] The data show the purified amount of chemical fertilizers.
[c] Foodgrain production here means yearly production. The national average here has been obtained
    by multiplying the per mu production by multiple crop index.
[d] "Gross rural social production" means total value of products of all rural material production
    sectors represented in amount of currencies. It includes productions of all cooperative
    economic organizations at the level of township, village, and below, as well as the production
    of various trade run by rural households, including agriculture, industry, construction,
    transportation, commerce, and catering. The total farming production of state farms are also
    included. However, production of state and county enterprises are not included.
[e] Data of the three counties are calculated according to the work reports of their respective
    Bureaus of Transport and Communications.
[f] County data derived from the 1992 work reports of the Irrigation and Water Conservancy Bureaus
    of the three investigated counties.
[g] The regional average of the area where the county locates. The national average is the result
    of the 1982 general survey.
[h] The data for infant mortality of the three counties has been provided by the family planning
    committees of the respective counties, while the number for national average is the rural infant
    mortality of 1986 (see Institute of Population Research, CASS [1988, 337]).

... = Data not available.

the province, focused mainly in the energy, transportation, and chemical industries. As a result, not only new lots of production capacities of coal, oil, electricity, ethylene, soda ash, and others were created, but handling capacities of harbors and telecommunication services were also markedly improved and transportation networks enlarged, thus adding wings to the economic development of the province (Research Office of Shandong Provincial Committee of Chinese Communist Party 1986; Shandong Provincial Statistical Bureau 1991).

However, similar to the situation of the whole nation, amid cheers of economic take-off, there also exist in Shandong Province underdeveloped corners. The Yimeng Mountain Region in mid-south Shandong represents one such example. Among the 12 counties in the region, 9 are poor counties with special support from the state and another poor county with special support from the province. The socioeconomic indices of all the 12 counties lie below the level of the provincial average. Due to poor traffic facilities and a shortage of water resources, the region has found itself difficult to develop in either farming or nonfarming sectors. By the end of the 1980s, 610,000 rural households with a population of 2.28 million people, representing 31.7 percent of the total population of the mountain region and 2.7 percent of the population of Shandong Province, still earned an average yearly income of less than 300 RMB yuan (Shandong Provincial Planning Commission 1990). The area and rural population of Yimeng Mountain Region account roughly for 11 percent of the provincial total. Compared with poor regions of other medium-developed or less-developed provinces, the aid in terms of investments given to Yimeng region in recent years has been more intensive, with most of the Yigong-daizhen projects in Shandong Province having been implemented here. For carrying out such public works, the local governments contributed matching funds to the size exceeding the proportion of 1 to 1.5 as compared with the value of invested goods put in by the Central Government (Table 3.2). The water conservancy investments only made by the province during the 1986-1989 period provided more than 100 million yuan to the project areas, more than 2 million yuan every year for every county, on average, triplicating the average level of the province. Comparatively stronger economic strength enabled the public works in Shandong Province to approach more closely the standard of regular capital construction. Competent authorities of Yigong-daizhen project for road construction stressed: "construct no substandard roads: Every road be up to standard" (Shandong Provincial Planning Commission 1990), showing obviously that the people engaged in the relief works had kept in mind the long-term economic growth of the area.

NINGXIA HUI MINORITY AUTONOMOUS REGION

Eight of the 16 counties of Ningxia Autonomous Region of Hui Nationality are poor counties situated on the loess plateau of southern Ningxia, known as the "Xihaigu Area." The area caught the attention of the Chinese Central Government in 1982, due to its heavy population pressure and the rapidly deteriorating ecological environment, and, together with the neighboring Dingxi and Hexi areas of Gansu Province, was able to be included in the special program of agricultural development known as the "3-Xis" Special Program ("3-Xi" in Chinese means the three areas of Xihaigu, Dingxi, and Hexi), thereupon becoming one of the earliest Chinese poor regions to obtain large-scale assistance from both home and abroad. Main contents of the "3-Xis" program include grass and tree planting projects, vegetation restoration projects, water conservancy projects, (including the diversion of the Huanghe River for irrigation purposes), the building of terraced fields, agricultural extension and training projects, organized immigration with the purpose of easing the population pressure, and so forth. To carry out the program, the Chinese Central Finance has allotted, every year since 1983, a special sum of 200 million yuan, equivalent to 7.14 million yuan, on average, for every county within the project areas.

Unlike Shandong, the poverty alleviation projects in Ningxia have been relying almost fully upon the inputs from outside. Although there are fertile and irrigated farms along the Huanghe River in the northern part of the autonomous region, and an energy industry with a long tradition as well, due to the price control under the system of central planning in the past, all the enterprises concerned have long been in a state of either low profit or even making losses. So it is too hard a job for the provincial north to compensate

the severe poverty of the Xihaigu area in the south, with their meager revenue. The eight poor counties in southern Ningxia, with a total area representing 58.8 percent of the whole Autonomous Region, have been inhabited
by 64.1 percent of the population of Hui nationality in Ningxia and 43.8
percent of the total population of the Autonomous Region. Being an arid
land, the annual rainfall here measures only 240-600 millimeters, on average, while the annual evaporation reaches 2,100 to 2,300 millimeters, on
average. The yield of farm production in the area has been markedly lower
than the national average, with the foodgrain production remaining at the
level of approximately 100 kilograms per mu per year. As a sharp contrast,
the population of the area grows rapidly. It showed a 2.14-fold increase
during the period from 1949 to 1982 and its natural growth rate reached
2.38 percent in 1991, higher than the national average level. Facts show that
the policy of family planning makes little effect in this Hui nationality inhabited area (Ningxia Autonomous Region of Hui Nationality, Agricultural
Construction Committee 1992).

Population growth—expansion of farmland—worsening environment—
intensified poverty—such a vicious circle has clearly manifested itself in the
Xihaigu area. The fuel problem of rural families represents one of the typical examples. Farmers here relied on turfs and grass roots as their main
source of fuels before 1982. Thus, year after year, they dug and shoveled to
root out grasses wherever possible, only to the result of continuous increases
of bared loess land, the ever serious soil erosion, and the more frequent
natural calamities. And even until now, the area remains in a state of "nine
years of drought in a decade," as the local people have described it. The implementation of the "3-Xis" program has been able to mend, to a certain
degree, the ecological environment of Xihaigu area and raised, initially, its
capacity in resisting natural calamities. And, what is more important, the
implementation of the program has partially eased the difficulties of the local poor in the shortage of foodgrains, fodders, and fuels, thus gradually
getting the activities undermining the vegetation under control.

However, once wrecked seriously, the environment is not easy restored in
a short period of time. Constantly hit by drought, the rural households in
Xihaigu area are still facing the difficult problem of drinking water short-

ages and are still in an awkward predicament of continuous output reduction and foodgrain shortages. Such a situation gives the Yigong-daizhen projects, in Ningxia a clear feature of "rescue operation" against natural calamities. On the one hand, farmers taking part in the works can partly compensate their losses in crop failures with their earnings from the relief works, to buy foods and other daily necessities, and on the other, the irrigation projects constructed can alleviate their drinking water difficulties while the roads built can benefit directly the transportation of relief goods and materials. The incident in 1973 is an example: it was a year of serious drought when 30 percent of the sheep in the area starved to death due to difficulties in the transportation of relief grass fodders. However, no death of cattle was reported in 1987, yet another year of serious drought, only because now roads had been built up and timely transportation for grass fodders became available (Ningxia Traffic Bureau 1992).

SICHUAN PROVINCE

Speaking of Sichuan, people may, first of all, remember its good reputation of a "heavenly land of abundance." It would be difficult to imagine that one-fifth of the counties in Sichuan Province are poor counties and about one-tenth of its population are poor people. In view of the fact that the population of Sichuan Province total 108.87 million people, these are not negligible percentages, showing that the poor population in Sichuan Province equals the total population of a small country in Europe, Hungary, for instance. As a matter of fact, the so-called "heavenly land of abundance" depicts the situation in the Chengdu Plain which only constitutes roughly 2 percent of the total area of Sichuan Province. Of the vast expanse of 570,000 square kilometers of Sichuan, 78.8 percent are mountain areas and plateaus and the remainder is hilly land. The 48 poor counties of the whole province scatter mainly in the Qinling, Daba, Wuling, and Wumeng mountain areas along the borders of the Sichuan basin. Besides, there are another three less-developed areas inhabited mainly be small nationalities. These are the Ganzi Autonomous Zhou (or prefecture) of Tibetan Nationality, the Aba Autonomous Zhou of Tibetan and Qiang Nationalities, and the Liangshan Autonomous Zhou of Yi Nationality, which include, altogether, 46 counties and a population of 5.24 million people (Statistics Bureau of Sichuan Province 1992). Special funds supporting the three areas have been arranged by the state.

Different from the practice in Shandong and Ningxia, where the Yigong-daizhen projects are concentrated in mainly poor counties, the projects in Sichuan Province extend to more than 70 counties in the mountain areas, in addition to the 48 main poor counties. It means that the projects in Sichuan are spread over an area constituting 57 percent of the whole countryside of the province (Sichuan Provincial Office for Yigong-diazhen Projects 1989). The reasons for this policy of Sichuan may be explained as follow:

1. The state of poverty differs slightly among the counties on the mountainous borders. However, the identification of poor counties from the ordinary ones was only done according to one- year data in terms of the per capita annual income and foodgrain in 1985 (Chapter 2.1). In fact, under similar natural and socioeconomic environments, counties failing to be listed as the poor ones may find their rate of poverty being more or less the same as those having been listed among the main poor counties.

2. Counties inhabited mainly by small nationalities usually face problems of water shortages and traffic difficulties, so that there are eager demands among the local population for relief works to alleviate such problems; hence, the policy inclination in favor of these areas when arrangements are worked out.

3. The territory of Sichuan is carved up by high mountains, deep ravines, and a crisscross network of big rivers, making the building of roads and bridges extremely difficult. So, the problem of traffic difficulties has long been the number one headache of the province. Especially in the mountain areas where transportation still, to a large extent, relies on manpower, a local inhabitant cannot but carry on his back a basket for transportation purpose ever since being a teenager. Being carried day in and day out throughout one's life, the basket looks as though it is an inseparable part of the human body of the local population. Furthermore, to travel from a remotest county to the provincial capital takes a journey of three days by vehicle and the routes connecting the area with neighboring provinces are not easy as well. Such a situation not only stands in the way of exploiting the resources of the mountain regions but also hinders the integration of the economy of the central plains of the province into the national market. Under such circumstances, the building of roads in the mountain areas of Sichuan serves a dual purpose: the improvement of conditions of existence for the poor population and the promotion of economic growth of the whole province.

The multiple goal of Yigong-daizhen projects in Sichuan Province clearly manifests itself in the way of disposal of resources. First, it is embodied in the priority given to construction of roads. The amount of investments in road projects in comparison with that in drinking water projects shows a ratio of approximately 8:2. The reason for this lies in the fact that shortage of traffic and transportation facilities has long been the "bottleneck" of the economic growth of the province. Second, due to the wide spread of the public works in Sichuan and the limited funds available, it is impossible for the works here to have the same standard as the regular capital construction projects, just as what has been done in Shandong Province. To suit such local conditions, flexibility becomes a marked feature in the project designs. Take the drinking water projects as an example: the model, size, and quality standards of the projects are all decided according to the population density of the project area. Centralized water supply systems would be constructed for towns, market centers, or villages, while assistance would be given to individual rural households dispersively inhabited in high mountain areas for the building of small water pits. In road projects, resources are disposed even more closely, connected with the economic benefits of every different road: standardized roads for vital public ways, tractor-ploughing roads for lanes with less traffic, and pedestrian passages and suspension bridges for subways used by a small number of poor households, and so forth.

COUNTIES UNDER THE SURVEY

The Linqu of Shandong, Xiji of Ningxia, and Wangcang of Sichuan are all poor counties with special support from the state. They belong, respectively, to Yimeng Mountain, Xihaigu area, and Qinling and Daba Mountains, the three poor regions among the 18 less-developed belts of the whole nation.

LINQU COUNTY OF SHANDONG PROVINCE

Linqu County is located 180 kilometers south of Jinan, the provincial capital of Shandong, a distance of about three hours drive by bus. The county has an area of 1,835 square kilometers, among which 12.8 percent are plains, 31.3 percent are hilly land, and the remainder is mountain areas (Table 3.3). The poor population of the county is spread mainly in the mountain areas and the settlement districts of the reservoir immigrants.

The natural conditions here seem not that bad. The mountains are not high, with an average yearly rainfall of 700 millimeters, an average temperature of 12.4 degrees centigrade, an average sunshine time of 2,578.6 hours, and an average frost-free period of 191 days. The farming crops here are reaped twice every year. But, though such favorable natural conditions, the poverty incidence among the county's rural population remained at the high level of 64 percent by the year 1985 (Linqu County Government 1991). Analyzing the historical data of the county, one can find that the root cause of the high poverty incidence of the area lies in the overburdened resources aggravated by the overgrowth of population.

During the period of 1949-1979, the population of Linqu County doubled from 360,000 to 720,000 people and it grew further to 880,000 people by the year 1990, raising the population density of this semi-drought area to the level of 480 people per square kilometer. In contrast to the trend of population increase, the per capita area of farmland decreased in successive years—from 2.4 mu in 1957 to less than 1.0 mu in 1987 (Local History Compiling Committee of Linqu County 1991). To meet the ever increasing requirements for food, farmers had resorted to such measures as increasing the inputs of chemical fertilizers, renovating cultivating techniques, building water conservancy projects, raising the irrigation index from 7 percent to

Table 3.3—Public works in investigated areas, completed in 1985-1990

Programs	Shandong	Linqu	Ningxia	Xiji	Sichuan	Wangcang
			Provinces/Counties			
Total investments (million yuan)	104.6	8.77	142.8	17.9	759.5	18.5
Central Government	46.4	4.33	81.8	12.6	447.2	11.0
Local governments[a]	58.2	4.44	61.0	5.3	291.3	5.0
Farmers[b]	...	...	0.0	0.0	21.0	2.5
Farmers' labor inputs[c] (million workdays)	...	...	(40.0)	1.1	(400.3)	13
Newly built roads (kilometers)	11,500	205	2,156	140	5,372	95
Reconstructed roads (kilometers)	...	...	821	128	4,662	97
Waterways dredged (kilometers)	0	0	0	0	780	0.6
Number of public way bridges built	415	30	117	3	1,850	37
Number of pedestrian bridges built	0	0	0	0	34	1
Pedestrian passages (kilometers)	...	43	0	0	150	...
People and cattle reached with drinking water supply facilities:						
Population (thousand person)	581	112.3	268.4	29.6	3,871	112.7
Cattle (thousand head)	...	3.1	339.2	20.2	4,392	105.0

Source: Shandong Provincial Planning Commission (1990); Linqu County Government (work report) (1991); Agricultural Department of Planning Commission of the Ningxia Hui Nationality Autonomous Region (1992); Xiji County Government (1992); Office for Relief Works in Poor Regions of Sichuan (1989), (1991); Planning Commission of Wangcang County (1991).

[a] The data for Shandong Province include the capital invested by the farmers.

[b] The sign '...' indicates that data are not available.

[c] The farmers in Ningxia obtained a total reward of 100 million yuan, convertible to 40 million workdays, according to a rate of 2.5 yuan for every workday. In the case of Sichuan, the investment during the period 1985-1988 was 380 million yuan, with the input of labor on the part of the farmers being 200.62 million workdays. Thus, the proportion between the investment and the labor input are calculated, and the labor input during the period of 1985-1990 can also be derived by further calculation.

... = Data not available.

48.8 percent, and raising the multiple crop index of foodgrain from 149 percent to 172 percent, thus having more than doubled the average per unit area yield of foodgrain to reach the level of more than 470 kilograms per mu in the year of 1987.

But the over-exploitation of the farmland finally led to the aftermath of a serious soil erosion, with 60 percent of the soil of the whole county affected. Another even more direct aftermath was the new strain on water resources, with the problem of water shortages in mountain areas, inherited from history, further intensified. Shortage of water caused a shortage of vegetables and foodgrains, showing a strange circle of food insecurity of the poor population in the mountain areas. Another consequence caused by the overgrowth of population was the surplus in manpower. With a rural labor force of 350,000 people in the whole county, an individual laborer could cultivate slightly more than two mu of farmland, on average, and the farm work in a whole year needed only three months to complete, showing, obviously, a state of underemployment, which led, inevitably, to the low income of rural households.

However, it was exactly on the basis of this fundamental superiority of abundant labor resource that Linqu County carried out its poverty alleviation strategies around the two main subjects of households food security and income generation. The first measure was a large-scale farmland capital construction movement to increase the arable land. But the movement in the 1980s had no longer been the "reclamation of wasteland" by destroying forests as had been done in the past. Now the farmers built terraced fields on barren mountain slopes, planted shelter forests on mountain tops, developed fruit trees on mountainsides, and constructed stable and high yield foodgrain farmland at the foot of the mountains. Besides, round-the-mountain roads and coordinating works for irrigation projects were also built up. All these showed that while reclaiming the marginal land, protection measures for ecological environment had been taken.

During the period from 1985 to 1990, in the whole county of Linqu, altogether 300,000 mu of slope land were terraced, 8 million fruit trees were planted, 40,000 mu of cultivated land were increased, 6,530 water conservancy projects were constructed, and 1,500 kilometers of round-the-mountain roads were built up. Funds for the purchase of necessary materials for the projects came mainly from the governments at higher levels, as well as assistance from international organizations and loans from banks, besides a small part of which taken from the turnover interests of the township enterprises or the financial accumulations of the village communities. Labor inputs were provided by farmers, free of payment. Ever since the year 1985, a total of 122 million workdays had been put in the farmland capital construction all over Linqu County, 348 workdays for every labor, on average.

Under conditions of family management of farming activities, such a large-scale collection of unpaid labor could be regarded as a special feature of the antipoverty strategy of Linqu County government. The feasibility of this practice lay mainly in institutional arrangements. First, the improved farmland would continue to be contracted to the farmers' households and the areas of the contracted land for an individual household would be in proportion to the workdays the farmer had put in. Second, it may be attributed to the implementation of the labor accumulation system, which stipulates that every rural labor must contribute, every year, no less than 50 workdays. The township government would make the assignments of contribution of unpaid workdays at the beginning of the year and the village committees would distribute the assignments to every household. The accounts would be settled at the end of every year. Those short of the assignments would pay, while those having overfulfilled the assignments would earn more. Such construction work has broken the territorial limits between townships and villages, with workday accounts also to be settled among different villages.

It has been a traditional practice for several decades in Linqu County to concentrate the labor force in slack farming seasons in order to carry out farmland capital construction. But, to turn such labor inputs into a generally acknowledged local means of payment was a new creation of the county government, which symbolized the common recognition of the system of labor accumulation. The background of this common recognition lay, first, in the farmer's expectations for more farmland under their respective managements and, second, in the low cash income of the rural households so that they owed no means of payments other than their own manual labor. Besides, there was a reason of cultural heritage. Being a revolutionary base during the 1940s, there had long been in the area a tradition of farmers putting their obligatory workdays in public undertakings.

The significance of Linqu County's practice of organizing large-scale investments in labor-intensive projects also lay in the transformation of surplus labor into a superiority of resources to replace, as much as possible, the capital investments, thus lowering the expense of the projects. Under such institutional backgrounds, the public works here naturally merged together with the comprehensive development programs of the whole mountain region. The drinking water supply projects carried out in the county since 1985 had solved the drinking water problems of 300 villages with a total population of 110,00 people. The more than 200 kilometers of roads at county and township levels, built under Yigong-daizhen projects, had effectively promoted the development of various commodity production and trades in the area.

Linqu County obtained from functional departments of the central government every year a fund totaling more than 11 million yuan for poverty alleviation purposes. Besides farmland capital construction, the funds have been used also in the development of fruit forests, breeding industries, and township enterprises, mainly of farm produce processing. A common feature of these invested projects was the utilization of local resources and the choice of labor-intensive techniques. However, the investments as stated above were not yet enough to absorb all the existing surplus labor. So, the county government also organized, through official channels, the local rural labor to work off-farm in Shanghai, in Shengli Oil Field of Shandong, and in the forest regions of Heilongjuang Province, with a total manpower outflow of around 50,000 people, which contributed markedly to the reduction of the poverty incidence. By the year 1991, the residents of the households with a per capita annual income of less than 300 yuan had decreased to less than 8 percent of the total rural population of the county.

XIJI COUNTY OF NINGXIA AUTONOMOUS REGION OF HUI NATIONALITY

Xiji County of Ningxia is far away from big cities, more than 400 kilometers apart from Yinchuan, the capital of the autonomous region, a distance of more than eight hours drive. With a population of 385,000 people, equally shared by the two nationalities of Hui and Han, the density of population of the county stands at 122 persons per square kilometer, well beyond the limit bearable for a drought area as such. According to the 1978 United Nations conference on desert encroachment, the population density of a semi-drought area should not be more than 20 persons per square kilometer and, for a drought area, the limit should not go beyond 7 persons per square kilometer (Zhang Yiming 1991).

Then the problem is, what accounts for the high population growth rate of Xiji County during the past 40 years or more? Besides the social stability and the improvement of the medical and health services, a decisive factor may lie in the system of food distribution by the size of households. Furthermore, the distribution of relief through civil administration organs has also been made with the similar principle, which stimulated the population growth from the same direction. All of these facts show that without a mechanism something like a "self-balancing apparatus" to control the proportion between the population and the resources, the improvement of social services will finally lead to the unexpected and disastrous result of rapid increase of population and the breakdown of the ecological equilibrium.

With an average elevation of 2,000 meters, an average annual temperature of 5.2 degrees centigrade, and an annual rainfall of less the 400 millimeters, the natural environment of Xiji County is unfavorable to farming activities. But up to now, the agricultural population of the area still constitutes 95.6 percent of the total population of the county (Table 3.3). By the end of the 1970s, the county had 1.9 million mu of land under cultivation, among which 80 percent were slope land with a foodgrain yield of 60 kilograms per mu (Xiji County Government 1992). Ever since the "3-Xis" construction program started, the World Food Programme has invested more than 22.8 million dollars in the county for grass and forest planting and terraced field building projects to turn 800,000 mu of cultivated land into grassland and forests, in addition to the special funds of the Central Government. By the end of 1991, the total area of cultivated land was 1.1 million mu in the whole county, half of which was constructed into terraced field and the remainder has still been the slope. By that time, per mu yield of foodgrain of the whole county increased to 101 kilograms, but there were still part of rural population in a shortage of foodgrain, which are filled up every year, at least, by 5,000 tons of "resold" or relief foodgrain (Xiji County Statistics Bureau 1990).

Because of the fragility of the local economy, the revenue of the county government has also relied on subsidies from the Central Government. Taking the year 1989 as an example, the subsidies Xiji County Government obtained from the Central Government was as much as 36.608 million yuan, while the local revenue of the same year was only 1.767 million yuan. The expenditure of the county government in the same year was 45.096 million yuan, among which 29.7 percent were for cultural and educational affairs as well as medical and health undertakings, and 4.3 percent were social welfare and relief expenses. It showed that social services in Xiji, though a poor county, were not that bad; the reason lay solely in the financial support of the Central Government (Chapter 4.1).

Such an economy, long relying on supports from outside, has not yet formed any point of growth, so far. The strategy of Xiji County Government is to bring about an overall economic growth through the establishment of enterprises processing peas, potatoes, and animal products. But, due to low output of the land and low productivity of the enterprises, only 3,000 job opportunities are expected to be created by these enterprises, still falling short of the expectations of the county government.

Projects having effectively provided short-term employment and income for the large amount of rural surplus labor and having gradually eased the situation of food shortages are construction of agricultural infrastructure, quite a number of which took the form of relief works. During the period 1982 to 1987, the World Food Programme invested a total of 43,325 tons of foodgrain in Xiji to be used for the payment of farmers working for the grass and forests planting projects. The Ministry of Civil Administration of the Central Government also provided for Xiji County, almost every year, relief funds and foodgrain, half of which were distributed to the poor taking part in the relief works, as their payments. So, whenever the State Planning Commission made assignments for road, water conservancy, and slope land transformation projects, the way of organizing such relief works had been no stranger to Xiji farmers.

The poverty alleviation projects, as such, have gradually shown their effects. The rate of poverty in Xiji County was as high as approximately 75 percent at the beginning of the 1980s, which had been reduced to 43.5 percent by the year of 1991, measured by the standard of per capita average income of 300 yuan and per capita average foodgrain ration of 300 kilograms of households (Xiji County Government 1992). The poverty line selected here was higher than that in the year 1985. It was because, according to the experiences of the investigated regions, only when this threshold had been crossed, did the food security of the rural households become stable. Otherwise, the households which had been extricated from poverty, according to official standards, would easily go back to the state of poorness once a natural calamity took place.

What is noteworthy is that the population growth rate of the county has long been standing at the level of around 2 percent. There are about 30,000 farmers here, traveling every year to even more remote places as Qinghai and Xinjiang to do odd jobs, showing that they know clearly about the problem of unemployment in their hometown, due to the over-growth of population and the shortage of farmland. However, because of their specialties in religion and culture, their feelings against the family planning policies have been stronger than farmers in other investigated counties. However, casting aside all other factors, the high growth rate in population would only hinder Xiji County from getting out of the vicious circle of poverty, or would even undermine again the gradually improving ecological environment. So, it has become imperative to combine the birth control measures with the relief programs.

WANGCANG COUNTY OF SICHUAN PROVINCE

If we classify the present economy of Linqu County as one tending to grow upward, and define the economy of Xiji as a subsidized one, then Wangcang County of Sichuan is just at the stage of a subsistence economy. By the end of 1990, more than 90 percent of rural households of the entire county had a per capita annual foodgrain output of more than 300 kilograms (Wangcang County, Office for Poverty Alleviation 1990), showing that the complete settlement of the problem of food shortage can be anticipated in the near future, the problem now still puzzling the county government and the local farmers, is how to increase the cash income of rural households.

The main factor restraining the income increase of farmers in Wangcang has long been traffic difficulties. Located at the bordering area of the three provinces of Sichuan, Shaanxi, and Gansu, the county is far away from the trade centers of all three provinces. Although the distance between Wangcang and Chengdu, the provincial capital of Sichuan, is only about 500 kilometers, it takes 11 to 12 hours to arrive by bus, because the journey crosses over mountains after mountains. The total area of the county amounts to 3,004 square kilometers, among which 70 percent are mountain areas, 20 percent are plains land, and the remainder, the water surfaces. The terrain of Wangcang County undulates drastically, with the biggest difference of height between mountains and plains being approximately 2,000 meters. In the year 1984, the density of roads of the whole county was 35.1 kilometers per every hundred square kilometers. As a result of the implementation of public works in road projects, the density increased to 41 kilometers per every hundred square kilometers. Even so, the problem of traffic difficulties in mountain regions had not yet been fundamentally solved. Farmers living in high mountain areas (more than 1,000 kilometers above sea level) must travel the whole journey to and from the market, carrying all their goods and commodities on their backs, to sell foodgrains or pigs and buy chemical fertilizers or daily necessities. The hardships faced by the local farmers in making travels and transportation and the high transportation charges for farming and industrial products cannot but adversely affect the competitiveness of local enterprises.

With a mild climate and plentiful rainfall, the average annual temperature of Wangcang County stands at 16 degrees centigrade and annual rainfall at around 1,200 millimeters. However, there also exists the problem of water shortages. Of the total population of 430,000 people, 45 percent have been concentrated in the narrow stripes of plain lands along the deep ravines. A large population with limited lands, the situation has led to the large-scale reclamation, during the past several decades, of the surrounding hilly lands, up to tens of thousands of mu in area, for foodgrain growing fields. The aftermath of such reclamations was the serious destruction of forests and soil erosion. Besides, there are a number of coal mines and smelteries spread out along this narrow corridor area. Without necessary measures for environmental protection, the original water sources have been contaminated by the wastes of these enterprises, thus intensifying the scramble for water between the mining and farming sectors.

The area of cultivated land in Wangcang County totals 295,000 mu, nearly half of which are spread on the mountain slopes, 800 to 1,400 meters above sea level. Although there exists a considerable amount of surface water resources, but with limited irrigation projects, the situation of "fields lying high above while water lowing beneath" has made most of the cultivated land difficult to get irrigated, termed by the local farmers as the "rain-feed-fields." The area of effectively irrigated land makes up only 26.6 percent of the total cultivated land of the county and farmers in mountain areas have been constantly menaced by seasonal water shortages. The drought season comes every year during the six months of winter and spring, affecting not only farming crops but also the drinking water for animals and human beings alike. In villages where no drinking water setup has been constructed, it takes at least 5 to 6 hours every day for a labor from each household to look for and carry back water for their respective families.

The background hidden behind the problem of water shortages is the wreckage of ecological environment caused by the overgrowth of the population. Wangcang had been a scarcely populated area, with high mountains and thick forests, and, hence, was once the base area of the Red Army and the revolutionary guerilla forces. During the years from 1949 to 1979, although the reclaimed land was expanded through the destruction of forests, from the hilly areas to the high mountains, the per capita area of cultivated land remained at the poor level of 0.8 mu, only because the population of the county also doubled in the same period. The ever-increasing heavy pressure of population finally awakened the local government to understand that, in order to extricate the people in mountain areas from poverty, the growth rate of the population must be reduced.

In the process of carrying out the policy of family planning, the Wang-cang County Government has worked out a series of effective measures and regulations, thus getting under control the natural growth rate of population, so that it remained at a yearly increase level of 0.7 percent during the 1980s (Table 3.2). What is more important is that by combining the family planning measures with the poverty alleviation programs, it has been able to change, gradually, the backward ideas and behavior of the poor, thus promoting the development of human resources:

1. It made use of night classes of village primary schools to enroll the adult illiterates below 40 years old for elementary education. It also set up "population schools" in every township to propagate basic knowledge of the family planning separately among different groups of people, such as un-married youth, couples at childbearing ages, breast-feeding mothers, and others. Besides, there were also training courses in various townships to popularize applied farming techniques, including silkworm breeding, pig raising, orange and tangerine growing, and others. The township govern-ments stipulated that young people could get their marriage certificate only when they had obtained their respective certificates for nonilliteracy and for the completion of the family planning training courses. It also stipulated that a married couple could get permission for having a child only when any one of the two had obtained the qualification paper of the farming technical training course. At a time when there has not yet been an effective means in China to promote rural compulsory education, this practice of Wangcang County, undoubtedly, has served as a kind of such compulsory education for the adults.

2. The county government also worked out a system of distributing birth quotas, to encourage poor households to develop production and make ef-forts to extricate themselves from poverty. The birth quota for the whole county was set by calculations according to the expected population growth rate. Then, the first distribution would be made among the townships, con-sulting the different sizes of their respective population, followed by a fur-ther distribution among households through the family planning supervision system at the township and village levels. In mountain areas, the model of two-children families was adopted, while in plain areas, the principle of one child for one family was insisted upon. For farmers in different areas and expecting a different number of times of birth, the county government raised different requirements on levels of foodgrain production and per capita annual income, thus setting an economic boundary, to prevent the income of relevant families from fall below the poverty line because of population increases. The county government regulation meant that even if a family in mountain areas had only one child, and even if a couple in a plains area had no child as yet, they would not get the birth quota if they failed to reach the required economic level. In such cases, the township governments or village committees would appoint specific cadres to keep in contact with these households and take measures to give them the necessary support, including priorities in granting discount loans, in supplying farming materials, in the implementation of projects of diversified economy, in arranging job opportunities in poverty alleviation enterprises, and in giving opportunities to learn yield promotion techniques in farming schools for free of charges, and so forth. When the economic capacity of these households had been enhanced to reach the set standard, the birth quota would finally be given. However, families having fulfilled their birth quotas would get no more additional quotas, no matter how high their incomes had become (Wangcang County, Family Planning Commission 1992).

3. The development of public welfare and social insurance undertakings. The county insurance corporation opened the old-age insurance program, while the villagers' committees had been continuously implementing the system of "five-guarantees household" (childless and infirm old persons guaranteed food, clothing, medical care, housing, and burial expenses), established during the time of "people's communes," thus encouraging farmers to change their traditional concept of "relying on more sons and daughters to provide for the old."

4. The extension of maternity and child care and the birth control services, including contraception, from county seats, towns, and townships, to the rural grass-roots units. Every village in Wangcang County established its own service room to promote, in coordination with the township medical centers, the system of premarriage medical examinations, the practice of modern midwifery, the maternity and child medical care, and the inoculating and vaccinating service for children below 7 years old. The county guiding station also dispatched professional personnel to make touring services to townships and villages, carrying with them advanced apparatus to do examinations for women at child-bearing ages and treat women's diseases. The improvements in basic medical and health services as such had kept the infantile mortality at a relatively low standard. During the period of 1987-1991, the all-county infantile mortality below 1 year old was around 2 percent (Wangcang County, Family Planning Commission 1992).

5. The establishment of education funds to support the children to go to school, which helped the rate of children at school among total school-agers of the county and the rate of primary school graduates to reach, respectively, the level of 98.6 percent and 97.4 percent. The practice had been for the purpose of enhancing the quality of the next generation through education.

6. To popularize the knowledge of eugenics and eradicate the old custom of close relative marriages. Training courses for matchmakers were arranged once every year, telling them not to go between males and females for early marriages or near-relation marriages. For close relatives having been engaged, enlightening education would be made in an effort to break such engagements and help them to find other partners.

The practices described above are clearly a combination of educational and compulsory measures and also a combination of long-term efforts (reflecting in the improvement of social services) and short-term arrangements (manifested in the system of birth quota distributions). The purpose of these measures lies in that restraining the birth behaviors of this generation in order to leave a sound environment for the living of the next generation.

In carrying out its antipoverty strategies, the Wangcang County Government has been able to, on the other hand, grasp the key link of regulating the relation between the population and the resources, and, at the same time, fully utilize the opportunities brought about by different kinds of poverty-alleviation programs to build roads and bridges, dredge waterways, plant forests, terrace farmland, raise irrigation and drinking water projects, improve soil of farmland with medium-or-low yields, and diffuse new farming

technics, thus having initially improved the local infrastructure and the ecological environment, and having extricated most of the farmers' households
from the predicament of food shortages. At present, while implementing
continuously these programs, the county and township governments are energetically promoting the development of the industrial enterprises and the
diversified economy of the households so as to foster the points of growth of
the local economy and increase the cash income of the farmers.

Comparing the socioeconomic conditions of the three investigated counties, one can find that the common difficulties of the three are the rapid
growth of population and the worsening ecological environment, the incon-
veniences in traffic facilities and the ill-informed circumstances, and the
unstable food security and low income of the farmers. However, due to different natural and socioeconomic conditions, the extent of seriousness of the
counties differ markedly with one another. Although all three are main poor
counties supported by the state, they still can be classified into three categories of common poor, medium poor, and the poorest. It is exactly because of
this that the antipoverty strategy of each of the three county governments
has its own characteristics. The practice of Linqu County has been characterized by the combination of outside assistance with local resources and by
the utilization of the labor accumulation system to advance the agricultural
infrastructure, to adjust the economic structures, and to create job opportunities. By so doing, the county not only has solved the problem in obtaining
food security for most of the population, but also created the possibility of
economic growth. The government and farmers of Xiji are still fighting the
food shortages with immense outside support, but the way out for the re-
moval of the absolute poverty, by relying on local resources, has not yet
been found. The poverty alleviation strategy of Xiji County is characterized
mainly by the gradual improvement of ecological environment through the
returning of farmland to forests and grassland. Its achievements has been
manifested, first of all, in the stoppage of the disruptive activities of the
farmers against the ecological environment. As a particularly poor county,
there exists, still, a long way to go for Xiji to enter the track of economic
growth. The practice of Wangcang County Government is typical of its
complete set of family planning regulations. The combination of the imple-

mentation of poverty alleviation programs with the control of population growth and the promotion of improving population quality is worthy to be regarded as a meaningful effort in human resource development, which also shows that the county government has grasped the key link of the whole work of poverty alleviation. However, lacking a favorable economic environment for growth, as Linqu has had, Wangcang has not yet extricated itself from the limitations of an economy of subsistence, though not threatened by the shortage of food as before.

The betterment, in recent years, of the conditions of subsistence of the poor of the three counties and the marked reduction of their respective poverty incidence shows that the efforts of the Central Government in making concentrated and comprehensive inputs of capital, technologies, and materials are effective. The program of public works, as one of the many supporting investments, has lost no time in merging into the socioeconomic development programs by the three county governments and to be used to solve the three major and difficult problems of the fragile infrastructure, the shortage of food, and the insufficient employment and low income of farmers. So far, although the problems of all three counties have not yet been completely solved, progress has been achieved to varying degrees after all (Table 3.3).

ORGANIZATIONAL PATTERNS OF YIGONG-DAIZHEN WORKS

The program of Yigong-daizhen (public works) in China has been organized through the traditional system of planning economies. So, the rules concerning the allocation and use of materials, the making of investments, the financial controls, and the duties of local governments and relevant functioning departments are all stipulated by the State Commission of Planning. Hence, there are similarities in the way of planning, controlling, organization, and supervision among different programs in different places.

The implementation of public works involves quite a number of functioning departments, such as planning, finance, banking, commerce, purchasing and marketing, agriculture, water and electricity, transportation, tax revenue, audits, public security, and others. Thus, only under close coordination among all relevant departments can there be an ensured supply of funds, materials, and laborers, and the programs can go ahead according to the plans. For this reason, leading groups for Yigong-daizhen projects are established in all local governments concerned at the provincial, prefectural, and county levels, to coordinate the works in different departments. The executive organs of the projects are the headquarters especially established for the implementation of each of the projects, composed of technicians of relevant professional departments (for example, bureaus of transportation, water conservancy, agriculture, and so forth), financial control personnel, and leading members of townships where the projects are located. During the course of construction, the township governments take the responsibility of mobilizing the labor force, making the requisition of land, dismantling the buildings thereon and removing the inhabitants, while the professional departments concerned are responsible for the administrative works of the construction.

The process of the confirmation of a project starts from the township government raising the application, to be followed by the bureaus of transportation and water conservancy of the county to examine, separately, the sub-applications involving matters within the scope of their respective businesses and to report their choices to the county leading group for examination and approval. If approved, proposal papers will be prepared by these professional departments to be forwarded successively to the departments concerned at the prefectural and provincial levels, for further examination and approval. This procedure of making applications is, in essence, a process of screening the proposals of lower government departments by the higher level departments concerned and of working out the plan of making investments. However, the final formula of the program must be approved by the provincial planning commission, then be transmitted downward to the county leading group, also through successive levels.

The principles of local governments at various levels in the selection of projects are giving priority to the easier ones; making concentrated efforts to ensure the most important ones; and carrying out the projects in stages. For road projects, the principles of effectiveness are stressed and the priority of investments are given to the following categories of projects: (1) feeder lines linking villages and towns with main roads; (2) transportation lines in areas with rich resources, but without accessible roads; (3) roads connecting existing public ways and transportation networks; and (4) renovation projects for existing roads with busy traffic, but poor in technical standards.

Drinking water projects are selected with the prerequisite of having necessary water sources and reliable technical materials. Following categories of projects have the priority of being selected: (1) projects with bigger portion of labor investment; (2) supplementary works for existing projects; (3) projects applicated by villages where the leading body has comparatively high organizational efficiency and the households voluntarily engage in the collection of funds or voluntarily contribute their labor inputs; and (4) water supply projects in townships or villages suffering seriously from water shortages.

According to the stipulations of the Ministry of Water Conservancy of 1984, water shortage at present day indicates the situation that villagers must go more than one kilometer in a single journey or climb a vertical distance of more than 100 meters to fetch water. And the standard marking the extrication from the drinking water difficulties, also according to the stipulations, has been laid as follows: during drought seasons, there should be a per capita daily water supply of more than 10 kilograms in northern regions and more than 40 kilograms in southern regions. For big cattle, there should be a daily water supply of 20 to 25 kilograms per head. And for pigs and sheep, a daily water supply of 5 to 20 kilograms per head. In areas with an average rainfall of below 600 millimeters, where dry wells and dry pits are usually used, it is necessary to keep, every year, a water storage sufficient for the consumption of two years. In the southern regions, there should be a reserve capable of ensuring the drinking water supply, even if there is no rain during a span of 70 to 100 days.

There are two kinds of laborers necessary for construction work: skilled and the unskilled labor. The former includes masons, carpenters, blacksmiths, and others who possess traditional skills. In recent years, they usually organize themselves into crews of contractors to contract works with higher technical requirements, not only in local construction work, but also in those in the outside counties. The latter are recruited local farmers engaging mainly in the physical work, such as removing the earth and stones. The earth- and stone work in road projects are usually contracted out by the project headquarters to the villager groups along the lines; it is the heads of the villager groups that distribute the works further to the households, according to the number of laborers of every household. The labor inputs of farmers contain, to some extent, the compulsory contribution which are embodied in the unpaid labor having been converted into the matching funds of the local governments for the investment by the central government. So far as this part of labor bears the nature of compulsiveness, the households possessing labor but unwilling to go to work must pay an amount to the villagers' group to relieve themselves from the obligations. However, due to the tradition of mutual supervision among village community members to make labor inputs for public benefit undertakings, such cases of preferring payments rather than going to work are very seldom. As for the drinking water projects, which will belong to individual households or village communities after their completion, all the unskilled work contributed by the villagers are rewardless and only the skilled workers therein are to be paid.

The labor payments are reckoned by task rates by the project headquarters, with the tasks being set according to the amount and difficulty of the work contracted. The daily payment of a skilled worker usually doubles that of an unskilled worker. The way of making the payments varies with the kind of materials the Central Government has allocated. When foodgrains, cotton, and cotton cloth are used as the inputs, then the payments for the project participants will also be made in the same kind of materials. And while stocks of industrial products are put in the construction works, what the farmers will draw will be the "industry coupons," which have the same value as the official currency of RMB functioning as if a kind of banknote to be used only once for all. The industrial coupons are to be used within the limits of their respective counties and only in the shops of state-owned departments of commerce, agricultural machines, and production materials, as well as in the county and township Purchasing and Marketing Cooperatives (Zhu Ling 1990).

The supervision, test, and acceptance of the projects are carried out by the professional departments taking charge of the engineering and technology works. The roads achieving grade 4 and above of the state technical standard would be brought into the road maintenance plan of the county. The newly built drinking water installations are to be controlled by the users themselves, while the villager committees would work out rules for the use of water and practice necessary supervision.

The whole process of planning, controlling, organizing, and supervising the public works, except the additional procedure of using the industrial coupons, has been the operational pattern for many years of the centralized planning economy system, well-known to the administrative cadres and the functioning departments of the governments at all levels, so that the organization of the program has been fundamentally effective. However, the process has also brought about the main disadvantages of the planning economy.

The strict restrictions of the competent authorities at higher levels on the orientation of investments made it difficult for the county and township governments to flexibly dispose of the resources according to local urgencies, while the village communities have been excluded from the decision making process. Thus, the programs approved at higher levels sometimes were not necessarily the projects urgently expected by the local governments and people. For example, the traffic inconvenience ranks first in Wangcang County among all its difficulties and the local government and people harbor a strong desire for road project investments. But the 1991 plan of public works of the county, approved by the higher-level authorities, regulated that most of the funds should be used in the construction of terraced fields, while the road projects took only a smaller portion of the investments. Thus, some villages in the county, not accessible by roads, obtained projects for the construction of terraced fields. A few individual village communities acted on their own to use the funds approved for terraced fields to build simple roads leading to areas outside the mountains, which resulted in conflicts with the authorities concerned and responsible for the terraced field construction. Finally, the relevant investments having been used were converted into debts owed by the village communities and the village committees concerned were instructed to fulfill the task of constructing terraced fields on time and with funds to be collected by themselves.

Besides, the process shows that programs of pubic works correspond to the investments in kind made by the Central Government in the infrastructure construction in poor counties. So, the main purpose of the local governments in carrying out the programs is, first of all, to create conditions for economic growth, with the provision of additional job opportunities and incomes for the poor being only their secondary aim. This is why there exist no targeting mechanisms in the operational process of the programs to select the poorest people to take part in the public works. Furthermore, with the program of Yigong-daizhen transferring gradually into long-term measures in support of the poor counties, certain local governments and professional departments concerned tend to adopt more capital-intensive technologies and employ more contractor crews so as to facilitate control of the projects, thus reducing the short-term job opportunities for the large amount of the poor and losing, gradually, the original meaning of the program of relief works.

Figure 3.1-Survey provinces of The People's Republic of China[a]:
Shandong, Ningxia, and Sichuan

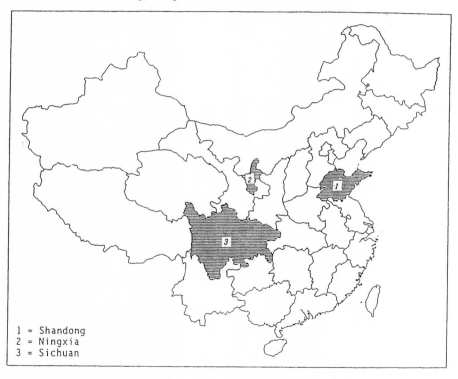

1 = Shandong
2 = Ningxia
3 = Sichuan

[a] Islands in the South China Sea not shown on map.

Figure 3.2-Survey counties

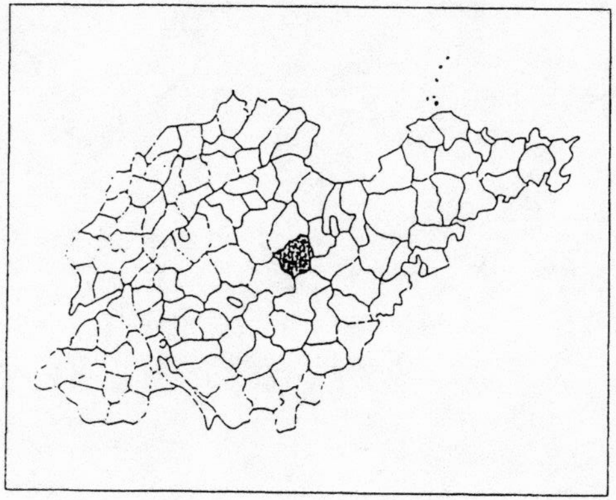

Xiji, in Ningxia Province

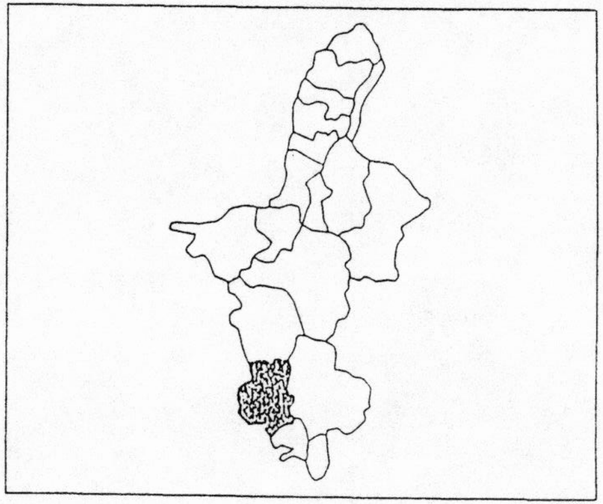

Linqu, in Shandong Province

Wangcang, in Sichuan Province

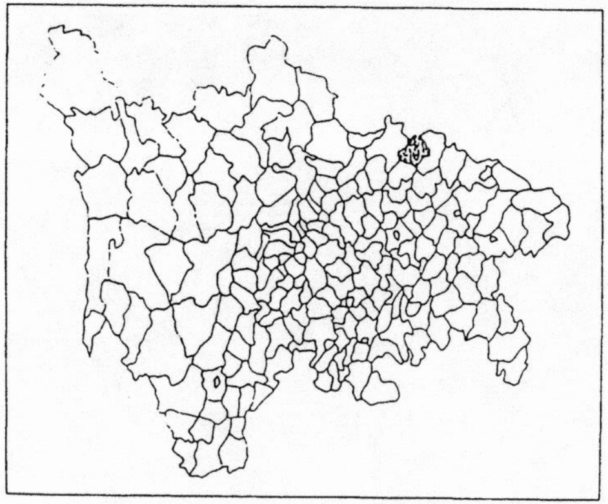

4

INFRASTRUCTURE OF SAMPLE VILLAGES

The main contents of this chapter comprise a statistics concerning the socioeconomic situation of the sample villages, a discussion on the state of social service setups therein, and an illustration of the part played by the village community organizations in carrying out the Yigong-daizhen projects.

VILLAGE COMMUNITIES

In the early 1980s, when the People's Communes were dissolved and the function of administration at the commune level was transferred to the township governments, the production brigades, an authority next to the Communes, were also abolished and a kind of self-governing body of villagers came into being in various administrative villages. Meanwhile, with the dying away of the production teams, the then basic accounting units of the People' Communes, the rural households of the former production teams, became independent producers, which organized themselves into villager groups as the grass-roots organizations of the newborn self-governing body of villagers. The transformations looked superficially like only a change of names of administrative institutions at different levels of the rural society. But in reality, with the background of the basic changes in the agricultural production system (that is, the replacement of the collective farms by the family farms) and the transition from a centrally planned economy to a market economy at macro level, these organizational changes in rural society had been imbued with substantial meanings. They constituted both a reorganization of the rural grass-roots societies to adapt themselves to the macro-structural transformations of the economy as well as a solid foundation for such a transition.

During the process of the transformation, the function of the village communities became more and more complicated. Here, the village community means a complex of such a rural grass-roots society as the administrative village, with the villagers' representative assembly being its self-governing organization and the elected villagers' committee being the executive organ. The tasks of a villagers' committee are, first of all, to distribute farmland of the village community among households and conclude contracts, playing a part of the landowner, with the individual households. As a legacy of the previous production teams, the land is now owned by the village communities. Under conditions when the market mechanisms are not yet available to regulate the land transfers, the practice of the village communities in redistributing land to meet the new requirements of the population changes and the structural adjustments of the rural economy can be considered as playing a role supplementary to the market.

The second main task of village communities is to provide services supporting agricultural production of the households, for example, the supply of improved seeds, plant protection services, irrigation, and so forth. The amount of the services provided differs from each other among various communities, due to their different financial availabilities. Besides, services of the public agricultural supporting systems (for example, the science and technology extension systems) are also provided for the farmers through the village communities.

Third, village communities have inherited from the People's Communes the function of social security by continuing the system of "five-guarantees" for the childless and infirm old or disabled persons. The communities also give assistance to the families of army men and revolutionary martyrs in their production work and livelihood.

Fourth, it is also the duty of the villagers' committee to administrate the cultural, health, and educational affairs of the community. Although there are government appropriations for these undertakings, due to the limits of the financial resource, the village communities must allocate extra funds to compensate the deficits (see Table 4.7). Taking the village primary schools and medical stations as examples, besides the charges they collected by themselves, there exist at least these two channels for the financial inflows.

Fifth, because the administrative network of the government has not been able to extend itself to the villages (with the township governments being the lowest level administrative organs), the village community organizations also play the role supplementary to the government administrative functions. All the rural policies concerned, no matter what it is, the family planning or the contracted purchases of government agencies, will be finally carried through to the households through the villagers' committees. So far as the poor regions are concerned, all the poverty alleviation programs, including Yigong-daizhen projects, rely on the villagers' committees to mobilize the participation of the farmers.

Then, where did the funds come from to meet the expenditure requirements of the village communities? Generally speaking, it came mainly from the fees they collected for the land use and the expenses apportioned among the households under different items similar to the community charges collected according to the number of family members. In the village communities with nonfarming enterprises, the turnover profits of the enterprises became the main source of the communities' revenue. Calculations on the correlations between the community revenue and the number of village enterprises in 1991 in the 34 sample villages selected for this research showed that the correlation coefficient between the two reached 0.7121, indicating that the village communities with more nonfarming enterprises enjoyed higher revenue.

So, it is not difficult to find that in the course of the rural economic reforms, the village communities have been transformed into self-governing units of the rural society. Their respective administrative organ, the villagers' committee, has emerged as a bridge between the government and the rural households, while exercising the function of disposing resources in areas where the market mechanisms remain incomplete.

SAMPLE VILLAGES

For the convenience of narration, the three investigated counties and 34 sample villages are here numbered, respectively, in a 5-digit code (Tables 4.1-4.3). The first digit of the code indicates the investigated counties, with "1" representing Linqu/Shandong, "2" representing Xiji/Ningxia, and "3" representing Wangcang/Sichuan. The second digit indicates village types: (1) villages participating in road construction projects; (2) villages with water supply projects; and (3) villages of the reference group. The third digit replaced the names of the sample villages, while the last two digits are used to differentiate the sample rural households in every sample village.

It has been known from previous case studies that the difference between the rich and the poor villages depend, to a large extent, on their different natural environment and infrastructure conditions. The selection of sample villages in this study has not been based on the average income level of rural households in various villages, but on the different categories of Yigong-daizhen projects in which the villages participated in 1991. The villages in first and second categories are those having participated in the road projects and drinking water projects, respectively, while those of the third category are villages not having been enlisted in the programs. However, so far as roads are concerned, villages not accessible by roads are usually low-income villages, rural households in villages newly connected with roads usually have more diversified income sources, while those having long enjoyed easy traffic facilities used to be the "rich points" in poor regions. Therefore, the sample villages selected according to different extent of participation in the projects can also reflect the gaps between the rich and the poor.

Tables 4.1-4.3 show the differences in the size of population among the sample villages, while Table 4.4 reflects their different economic conditions. It can be seen from the ratios of the labor force to the overall population of

Table 4.1—The profile of sample villages of Linqu/Shandong (the first county)[a]

Code	Village Names	Total Households	Population	Average Household Size	Number of Sample Households	Sample Population	Sample Population/ Total Population (percent)
11100	Shuang-Shanqian	188	739	3.93	10	39	5.3
11200	Xihuangshan	175	688	3.93	10	40	5.8
11300	Zengjiazhai	154	604	3.92	10	40	6.6
11400	Dagaojia-Zhuang	471	2,013	4.27	10	45	2.2
12100	Taoyuan	198	766	3.89	10	47	6.1
12200	Longnan	140	560	4.00	10	39	7.0
12300	Guoquan	135	478	3.54	10	43	9.0
12400	Xiashanzao	70	281	4.01	10	43	15.3
13100	Laozhuang-zi	100	410	4.10	10	47	11.5
13200	Jianyu	125	486	3.89	10	39	8.0
13300	Xujiayu	151	590	3.91	10	37	6.3
13400	Xujiawu	21	78	3.71	10	45	57.7

a The source of this table, and other tables as well, are taken from the authors' sample surveys, except those with special notes. The data represent the situation of the investigated areas in the year 1991.

Table 4.2—The profile of sample villages of Xiji/Ningxia (the second county)

Code	Village Names	Total Households	Population	Average Household Size	Number of Sample Households	Sample Population	Sample Population/ Total Population
							(percent)
21100	Maoping	216	1,276	5.91	10	52	4.1
21200	Subao	306	1,733	5.66	10	52	3.0
21300	Mengwan	261	1,539	5.90	10	52	3.4
21400	Wangping	367	2,217	6.04	10	52	2.3
22100	Majian	323	1,986	6.15	10	58	2.9
22200	Zhouwu	366	2,044	5.58	10	48	2.3
22300	Dacha	175	1,014	5.79	10	53	5.2
22400	Yanli	212	1,158	5.46	10	54	4.7
23100	Yaozichuan	198	1,204	6.08	10	51	4.2
23200	Yumu	200	1,152	5.76	10	43	3.7
23300	Shangma	213	1,242	5.83	10	55	4.4
23400	Yaozhuang	276	1,471	5.33	10	51	3.5

Table 4.3—The profile of sample villages of Wangcang/Sichuan (the third county)

Code	Village Names	Total Households	Population	Average Household Size	Number of Sample Households	Sample Population	Sample Population/ Total Population (percent)
31100	Lujiaba	281	1,121	3.99	10	41	3.7
31200	Longzhu	144	631	4.38	10	47	7.4
31300	Chunsun	233	973	4.18	10	43	4.4
31400	Youyi	93	366	3.94	10	49	13.4
32100	Xiangshui	496	1,796	3.62	9	37	2.1
32200	Huangyang	537	1,960	3.65	10	35	1.8
32300	Xiaosong	171	699	4.09	9	39	5.6
32400	Huashan	107	437	4.08	10	50	11.4
33100	Huya	345	1,347	3.90	20	81	6.0
33200	Lianhua	153	556	3.63	20	78	14.0

the sample villages that in the sample villages of the third county, the dependents take a smaller share in the total population than that of the labor force, and that in the sample villages of the second county, the share of the labor force in the overall population is lower than that in the other two counties. This indicates from the reverse side the higher dependent ratio in the county Xiji, which coincides with the narrations in the previous chapter on the demographic characteristics of the studied counties.

It is necessary to clarify here that the production structure of all the sample villages is of the same type, with planting being the dominant sector, but their respective main crops are different because of the limitation of natural environment. The main crops of the first county are wheat, maize, sweet potatoes, and tobacco, while those grown in large areas of the second county are potatoes and peas, followed by wheat and maize. As for the third county, it abounds in rice paddy, maize, sweet potatoes, and rapeseeds. Although all three are poor counties, some particular villages in the first and third counties still bear the task of fulfilling the foodgrain purchasing quotas of the state, though having been fixed at a very low level (except those villages belonging to the second category, which enjoy the facility of water supply systems). According to the previous surveys made by the authors, in the foodgrain-producing provinces in southern China, the average per mu state foodgrain-purchasing quota reached around 150 kilograms, at least. As the system of state foodgrain-purchasing quota is a government compulsory measure in collecting foodgrain, farmers can only dispose freely of their remaining foodgrain after completing their sales to the government, which had been fixed. The policy of the Central Government in poor regions in this regard is to reduce or to allow exemption from the purchasing quota. So, putting aside the considerations of trade volume, it can be said that within the scope of the control of the centrally planned system, the poor regions enjoy more freedom in trade than the developed regions.

The item of "area of gardens" in Table 4.4 indicates the areas of fruit gardens, tea plantations, or mulberry fields. The gardens in the first county are mainly newly established haw gardens and apple gardens, while the data under this item for sample villages in the second county are all marked as "0," because of the dry climate. The gardens in the third county are mostly mulberry fields, due to the silkworm breeding tradition of the local households.

Among the three categories of nonfarming enterprises, the village enterprises, the partner households' enterprises, and the individual industrial and commercial households, the last one is predominant in number and concentrates mainly in the retailers', catering and transportation sectors, characteristic of their small capital investment and their suitability for individual household management. So far as the relations with the village communities are concerned, there is no difference between the households engaged in either the individual industrial and commercial businesses or the partner households' enterprises, and the ordinary rural households. Although they are farming part-time, they are not to pay any tax concerning their nonfarming industrial activities to the village communities. This has been proved by the result of the correlation calculations between the village revenue and the number of the enterprises of these two categories: the correlation coefficient = -0.00039, with no significant relationship having been shown.

The sample villages are no more than 7 kilometers apart from their respective township centers. Only some remotest ones in the third county have a distance of about 10 kilometers. Township centers are political, economic, and cultural centers of various townships where not only the township government is located, but also the middle and primary schools, medical centers, post offices, monetary institutions, purchasing and marketing enterprises, agricultural technology extension and veterinary stations, and other rural service setups, even in remote mountain areas. The spread of the service setups as such is a result from the establishment of the administrative system under the planned economy, which undoubtedly have benefitted the development of the poor regions. The sites of the township governments are usually at the same time the market centers. Thus, the farmers living all around can use these facilities when they go to the periodical markets.

The observation on the social services at the village level has been conducted through inquiries concerning problems in six aspects. These are the existence of accessible roads (the possibility of driving a truck into the

Table 4.4—Basic economic situation in sample villages

Indicator	First County Category			Second County Category			Third County Category		
	1st	2nd	3rd	1st	2nd	3rd	1st	2nd	3rd
Cultivated area	1,173.8	505.5	417.0	3,460.8	4,446.3	5,944.5	748.8	593.6	1,127.5
Per capita cultivated land (mu)	1.0	0.9	1.1	2.0	3.0	4.7	1.0	0.7	1.2
Labor force (person)	401	255	215	769	585	411	450	660	492
Labor force/total population (percent)	44.0	47.0	51.0	45.0	38.0	32.0	59.0	55.0	49.0
Irrigated land/cultivated land (percent)	31.0	45.0	11.0	0.0	0.0	1.0	28.0	41.0	0.5
Average foodgrain purchase quota (kilograms per mu)	3	15	5	0	0	0	4	46	1.5
Area of gardens (mu)	147.5	87.5	37.5	0	0	0	103.5	173.5	575.0
Forest areas (mu)	15	17.5	426.3	35.5	12.5	556	5,407.5	657.5	1,000.0
Number of village enterprises	0	0	0	0.5	1	0	1.5	3.5	
Number of partner households' enterprises	0.5	0	0	1.5	0	0.5	0.8	3.3	0
Number of individual industrial and commercial households	21	2	1	17.5	14	2.8	14.8	25	1
Distance from township center (kilometers)	7	2	6	4	3	5	6	4	7
Distance from county seat (kilometers)	25	21	29	31	45	25	56	22	30
Distance from nearest bus station (kilometers)	0	2	13	2	1	5	3	4	11

Table 4.5—Infrastructure in sample villages

Indicator	First County Category			Second County Category			Third County Category			Overall Sample Villages
	1st	2nd	3rd	1st	2nd	3rd	1st	2nd	3rd	
				(percent)						
Villages accessible by roads/total sample villages	100.0	100.0	100.0	100.0	25.0	100.0	100.0	100.0	50.0	88.0
Villages with power supplies/total sample villages	100.0	100.0	100.0	100.0	100.0	25.0	50.0	100.0	100.0	85.0
Villages with purchasing and marketing stations/total sample villages	50.0	100.0	100.0	100.0	100.0	100.0	50.0	25.0	50.0	76.5
Villages with medical service/total sample villages	100.0	100.0	50.0	100.0	100.0	100.0	100.0	100.0	50.0	91.2
Villages with water supply points/total sample villages	100.0	100.0	100.0	100.0	75.0	100.0	50.0	100.0	100.0	91.2
Villages with primary schools/total sample villages	100.0	100.0	25.0	100.0	100.0	100.0	100.0	100.0	100.0	91.2

villages as a criterion); the availability of power supplies; the stores for purchasing and marketing farm products and inputs (improved seeds, chemical
fertilizers, pesticides, and so forth); medical service station; drinking water
supplies; and the village primary schools. Table 4.5 shows that 76.5 percent
of the sample villages have purchasing and marketing establishments, villages with accessible roads and power supplies constitute, respectively, 88
percent and 85 percent of the overall sample villages, while the sample villages with medical service, water supply stations, and primary schools make
up more than 90 percent of the total. It is, thus, evident that the coverage of
the social services in poor regions in recent years are considerably wide.
Taking the medical service as an example, villages with medical stations all
over the country constituted 86.2 percent of the total villages in 1990 (State
Statistical Bureau 1991), while, in this sample survey, the share reaches
91.2 percent.

In order to compare the situation of social services in the sample villages
with numerical indices, we vest every kind of service stated above with 1
point. Then, villages with all the six kinds of service facilities would gain 6
points. As indicated by Table 4.6, none of the sample villages gains "0"
points, with the lowest mark being "1" and those gaining 3.0 points and below making up only one-third of the total sample villages. The villages participating in Yigong-daizhen projects averagely gain 4.0 points while the
reference villages have 2.5 points at average. The differences could partly
be explained by the effects of the projects on village infrastructure, then,
what on earth are the other factors correlated with the provision of social
services? Separate correlation calculations for these villages between the
infrastructure points, on the one hand, and the village annual revenue (Table
4.7), the size of population, and the distance from the county seat, on the
other, showed that there exist only weak correlations between the provision
of social services and the annual revenue (correlation coefficient =
0.15443), and negative correlations between the provision and the distance
from the county seat (correlation coefficient = -0.18720), having no significant relationship in both cases. However, the results of the calculations give

Table 4.6-Distribution of sample villages by levels of provision of social services

Provision Level	Number of Villages	Share in Sample Villages	Accumulated Frequency	Accumulated Percentage
1	2	5.9	2	5.9
2	2	5.9	4	11.8
3	7	20.6	11	32.4
4	10	29.4	21	61.8
5	6	17.6	27	79.4
6	7	20.6	34	100.0

Table 4.7—Revenue and expenditures of sample villages, 1991

Items (yuan)	First County Category			Second County Category			Third County Category		
	1st	2nd	3rd	1st	2nd	3rd	1st	2nd	3rd
Turnover from last year	20,159	2,075	681	8,362	598	1,290	1,682	-2,500	-5,000
Current year revenue	47,699	32,899	10,598	...	3,931	5,736	14,327	206,792	6,755
Current year expenditures among which:	46,935	36,332	10,619	...	3,446	3,683	15,152	124,690	2,405
Public welfare undertakings	3,393	2,500	0	50	0	0	2,000	37,500	0
Primary school subsidies	713	1,378	88	40	920	25	88	725	540
Payments for village cadres	6,475	4,695	3,586	3,104	2,510	2,925	1,415	2,300	740
Turnover to next year[a]	20,922	-1,358	660	9,957	1,083	3,343	857	-40,583	-5,000

... = Data are not available.

[a] The fund to be turned over to next year was not equivalent to the gap between the revenue and the expenditures of the current year, because there existed deficits of some villages.

support to the fact that the provision of the most fundamental social services in Chinese villages has not been determined wholly by the wealthiness and the location of the village communities themselves, and that the spread of social service facilities as such is, to a large extent, the outcome of government interventions.

The calculations also tell that the provision of village infrastructure is not highly correlative with the population size of the villages (correlation = 0.23227), but the correlation has passed the significance test at the confidential level of 0.001. It means that the more dense the population, the higher the standard of social services. Similar finds have been made by Wanmali (1992) in his observations on the layout of the rural infrastructure in southern India. It is obvious, then, that the density of population is the decisive factor in the distribution of the rural social services, even under different economic systems. In circumstances of a market economy, when the settlements of local inhabitants have a considerable size, the payments made by the population for the services they enjoyed are possibly sufficient for maintaining the operation of the social service facilities. Meanwhile, in areas where the disposal of resources having been carried out through administrative measures, the principle of equal distribution according to population size also benefits, first, the village communities which are densely inhabited.

ROLES OF VILLAGE COMMUNITIES IN CONSTRUCTION OF PUBLIC WORKS

In the implementation of the Yigong-daizhen projects, the task of the village communities is to mobilize and organize labor force to remove earth and stones. According to the statistics based on the village questionnaires, the households taking part in the road projects constitute, on average, 60 to 70 percent of the total households of every village, with the ratio between female and male laborers being 2:3 (Tables 4.8 and 4.9).

Table 4.8—Labor input of sample villages in road projects, 1990

Item	First County Category			Second County Category			Third County Category		
	1st	2nd	3rd	1st	2nd	3rd	1st	2nd	3rd
Average number of households/village	246	135	100	205	37	...	130	252	168
Participating households	130	84	93	196	37	0	60	131	0
Male participants	133	75	119	330	40	0	69	127	0
Female participants	100	42	66	147	25	0	47	119	0
Workdays	10,613	3,549	8,825	7,757	1,762	0	7,510	8,973	0
Of which: obligatory workdays	7,708	2,548	8,825	269	0	0	591	5,800	0

... = Applicable original data not available.

Table 4.9—Labor input of sample villages in road projects, 1991

Item	First County Category			Second County Category			Third County Category		
	1st	2nd	3rd	1st	2nd	3rd	1st	2nd	3rd
Average number of households/village	130	136	101	284	...	...	130	301	173
Participating households	123	123	93	272	0	0	47	174	75
Male participants	136	110	126	329	0	0	61	158	90
Female participants	105	52	68	145	0	0	40	152	75
Workdays	11,650	2,240	11,045	8,081	0	0	18,797	9,150	2,500
Of which: obligatory workdays	7,213	2,182	8,350	340	0	0	344	4,923	2,000

... = Applicable original data not available.

Now, the problem lies in the fact that some cadres interviewed may have confused the road construction with the coordinating projects of passageways in the capital construction of farmland. Some others may have mistakenly included the labor inputs in other relief works (for example, drinking water projects and terraced fields construction) in the labor inputs in road projects. Thus, Tables 4.8 and 4.9 may not be able to clearly show the discrepancies between the sample villages of the first category (that is, the village communities taking part in road projects) and those of the other two categories in their respective inputs in road construction. However, these two tables can at least roughly provide the following information.

First, a comparison of the sample villages of the first category of the three investigated counties tells that such villages of the third county have the lowest average rate of households participating in the road projects (36.2 to 46.2 percent); those of the first county have the next lowest rate (52.8 to 94.6 percent); while the villages of the second county have the highest rate of participation (94.6 to 95.7 percent). However, further explanations are necessary because the sample village communities have been taken with administrative villages as the units, while the working units in road projects are villager group. Every administrative village covers more than one villager group. Some of them live together in nearby settlements, while some others are scattered all around in different settlements. In the three investigated counties, the second county (Xiji County in Ningxia) has a comparatively smooth terrain and its rural households are concentratedly inhabited. Usually, an administrative village there itself is a big settlement where rural households of several villager groups live together, so that, once tasks of road buildings are assigned to the villages, most of the rural households are able to easily take part, besides a few with particular difficulties (for example, the "five-guarantee households"). The situation in the first county (Linqu of Shandong) is more or less the same. But the conditions in the third county (Wangcang of Sichuan) are quite different, where the rural households live dispersively in the high mountain ridges. Even if the line of a road project is designed to pass through an administrative village, rural households of the villager groups belonging to the village are not surely in a

Table 4.10—Unpaid labor used in sample villages, in workdays, 1991

Obligatory Workdays	First County Category			Second County Category			Third County Category		
	1st	2nd	3rd	1st	2nd	3rd	1st	2nd	3rd
Per capita	11	6	26	0	0	0	1	2	2
Per male labor	22	1	27	0	0	0	4	8	1
Per female labor	9	0.5	19	0	0	0	4	5	1
Per mu	19	0.25	15	0	0	0	0	0	0
Amount used per village	7,067	1,105	2,140	0	0	0	2,203	5,720	2,117
Workdays per household put in water projects	0	51	0	0	0	0	16	23	0

position to take part in the works concerned, because, quite often, they are separated by mountains or rivers from reaching the construction sites. So, it can be said that traffic facilities constitute an important factor affecting the farmers' participation in the road projects.

With villager groups being the units in the implementation of the construction works, it is natural that the organization of the projects lacks the function of targeting at individual poor households. Furthermore, the village communities today remain so closed off that responsibilities set for village A would never be shared by village B and benefits flowing towards village B (for example, job opportunities created by road projects) are also difficult to be enjoyed by village A, even partially. Among the rank of laborers organized by the village communities in the implementation of the projects, the unskilled workers are all natives of local places, and possibly only technicians are invited from outside villages in times of shortages. So, the item "rate of households participation" in the tables cannot be equivalent to the rate of poor households taking part in the projects.

Second, in all the investigated counties, male participants are more than females (Table 4.10). The reasons for this lie in following two aspects. On the one hand, the payments for removing earth and stones are reckoned in task rates that are in favor of the males, due to their physical superiority, which results in higher efficiency. Hence, the preferences of the males to go to work. On the other hand, the labor division between the males and females in farmers' families determines that women will consume more time in housework, breeding, and fieldwork, which limit the extent of their participation in the construction projects.

Some foreign experts have strongly recommended the way labor recruitment contains a mechanism of "self-targeting," which manages to set the wages in public works at the level roughly equivalent to that in the farming sectors, so as to ensure the laborers recruited in the public works are poor people (Ravallion 1990). However, under the present situation of the socioeconomic organizations in Chinese poor regions, this method of recruitment may not be able to target the poorest and its transaction costs, perhaps, would be higher than those of the current operative patterns. The most mobile laborers in the Chinese countryside, nowadays, are not the poor, while the poorest used to confine their activities to their own villages or townships, because of their inability to pay traveling expenses. Though barriers among village communities obstruct the factor mobility, they also protect, at times, the local poor in obtaining short-term job opportunities, when a project is placed in a village or a township. Furthermore, payments for laborers working in public works are at the same level as those of the local unskilled workers, so there actually exist a function of targeting the poor. Viewing against this background, it becomes easier to understand the important role of the village communities in mobilizing the labor force and in the choice of the organizational patterns.

The statistics on the village sample show that about 4 percent of the villages have adopted the way of making personal contracts in the organization of laborers for the construction of public works, while 11.5 percent of the villages took the pattern of making selections by the villagers' committees, 7.5 percent of the villages offered no clear information about the way of labor mobilization, and the rest of the sample villages (77 percent) took the pattern of distributing the assignments of earth and stone works among the households by the villagers' committee according to the household size. The households with labor but unwilling to take part in the project must pay the amount equivalent to the wage of the local unskilled workers, thus enabling the villagers' committees to hire other persons to fulfill the work. Because it is the household that constitutes, finally, the unit taking part in the construction work, the labor division inside the rural families cannot but affect directly the extent of participation of male and female labor in the projects.

Third, the inputs of obligatory workdays in the road projects by the households of the first county were several times that of the other two counties, lending a support to the descriptions in Chapter 3.2 on features of the development policies of the county. The fact also indicated that massive labor accumulations had been made by the local farmers contributing to the construction of infrastructure.

Labor represents the richest resource in poor regions. While striving to achieve economic growth by making the best use of local resources under conditions of capital shortages, it is of key importance to substitute capital by labor as much as possible. Then, how did the village communities establish and carry out the system of obligatory labor input? And how did they replace the capital by labor in the construction of public works through this system? It has been learned through the questionnaire to village cadres that among the 34 sample villages, about 52.9 percent already set up this system, one-quarter of the total have not yet established, and another one-quarter have not answered the questions.

Table 4.10 shows that the villages have not yet established this system of concentrating themselves in the second county. Perhaps it is because the farmers in comparison with those in the other two counties are even poorer, so that they prefer lying idle to save their own calories, rather than putting in unpaid labor for public works. However, it is a worthy question further that drinking water supplying systems would be assets of village communities (or rural households) after their completion, with the state providing the building materials and the rural households contributing unpaid labor. Why then, did rural households of the second county not contribute obligatory workdays, even for such projects? There are generally two explanations for this. The first one lies in the far bigger relief funds, subsidies and capital investment the county obtained from the central government and the second one is the ineffectiveness of the county administrative system in organizing the laborers.

The amount of unpaid labor input of the rural households in the first county is the biggest among the three investigated counties. Calculations based on the average per village annual obligatory workdays used in the year of 1991 and the number of laborers reveal that the average amount of unpaid labor inputs of every laborer of the three different categories of villages are 17.6, 4.3, and 9.9 workdays, respectively. The results of the corresponding calculations for the third county are 4.8, 8.6, and 4.3 workdays, respectively. According to regulations of the State Council, the annual unpaid labor inputs of every rural laborer in the construction of roads, water conservancy projects, and other public facilities can be no more than 15 workdays. So, it is obvious that the obligatory labor inputs of the villages of the first county engaged in road projects have exceeded the maximum limit set by the State Council. The reason why the rural households here have

Table 4.11—Average daily wages for unskilled male laborers in investigated regions, in yuan, 1991

Working site	First County Category			Second County Category			Third County Category		
	1st	2nd	3rd	1st	2nd	3rd	1st	2nd	3rd
Home village	3	5	4	2.3	...	...	5.1	4.3	3
Native township	4.8	4.8	5	4	...	...	5.4	3.6	3
County seat	5	4.5	4.5	4.8	...	...	4.5	3.8	5
Provincial capital	3.5	2.5	3	6	...	...	5	6.3	4

... = Data are not available.

Table 4.12—Annual time use[a] of rural households in general, in days

Items	First County Category			Second County Category			Third County Category		
	1st	2nd	3rd	1st	2nd	3rd	1st	2nd	3rd
Crop production among which:	175	200	175	167	227.5	272.5	323.8	120	225
Peak season	55	85	57.5	92.5	140	141.3	137.5	62.5	120
Preparative activities	11.8	20	14.5	14	13	23.5	26	14.3	20
Marketing	12.5	22.8	12.5	7	14	13.5	73	60.8	15
House work	30	75.8	58	132.5	177.5	180	111.5	128.8	325
Non-workdays (1 male and 1 female)	217.5	136.3	130	185.1	122	110.1	83.1	83.3	27.5

[a] Original data taken from the experiential estimations of the leading members of different villages on the annual time arrangements of the medium size rural households in the villages concerned.

accepted such arrangements of the village communities may lie not only in their urgent needs for more roads, but also in the fact that the labor in these villages used to be left idle for more than three months every year (Table 4.12).

Table 4.11 has listed the data on the average wages per workday for unskilled male workers in the investigated regions, with its sources taken from the answers of the sample village cadres to the questionnaires. But the cadres knew best only the situations in their native villages and townships, while things of the labor market in the county seats and provincial capitals were quite strange to them. So, sometimes peoples from the same county offered discrepant information. For example, among the data provided by the third county on the level of wages in the relevant provincial capital, the gap between the highest and the lowest values was as big as more than two yuan. The average wage level of certain villages in the table were even higher than the level in the townships. The reason for this phenomenon lies in the fact that there were coal mines or other enterprises in such villages.

It is necessary to clarify that in the investigated regions, those frequently having an opportunity of unskilled non-farming employment are in the minority, while most of the labor are still not in a position to obtain such opportunities. This would be proved further in Chapter 6 in the statistics on income sources of the rural households, though data in Table 4.12 has already shown that the nonfarming activities of the sample households remain in an unimportant position in their annual arrangement of time. Each of the medium-sized rural households in the investigated regions has generally 2 to 2.5 labor and spare about one-third or one-half of their time annually for the crop production including pre- and post-production activities. Time consumed in house work for every household varies from 30 to 325 workdays annually, so big a span of difference reflecting possibly a misunderstanding in the concept of the term "housework." Besides the cooking, sewing, the care of the old and the young, the fetching of water and coal, the chopping of firewood and other activities directly relating to household consumption, some of the interviewees have mistakenly put the business of family breedings (pig raising, silkworm breeding, and so forth) in the category of housework. Though, through the questionnaire, the annual volume of leisure time of the male and female laborers in the investigated regions has been roughly made known, which is actually the foundation of the village communities to mobilize the rural households to lay their labor inputs in public works.

SUMMARY

During the process of economic reforms, the village communities have replaced the production brigades in becoming a kind of combined socioeconomic complex. Due to the fact that the ongoing institutional transformations have not yet extended the government administrative system down to the village level, so that the village community organizations are playing the role supplementary to the administrative functions of the government. In the economic field, due to the incompleteness in the market development, the village community organizations are also playing the role supplementary to the functions of the market in some areas of resource allocation. Up to now, most of the village communities have had the basic facilities in the supply of social services, among which the implementation of the Yigong-daizhen projects have effectively improved the traffic and water supply conditions of the village communities in poor regions. In the construction of roads and drinking water supply systems, the function of the village communities has been mainly the mobilization of the labor force to take part in the earth and stone works.

5

HOUSEHOLD AND INDIVIDUAL PARTICIPANTS OF YIGONG-DAIZHEN PROJECTS

In Chapter 4, we have already discussed general principles guiding village communities' mobilization of labor force to take part in Yigong-daizhen projects. What kinds of rural households and individuals are involved in the projects? What are the major factors determining their participation? All these are unknown to us. Chapter 5 tries to provide answers to these questions through quantitative analyses in order to clarify the beneficiary selection mechanisms of the projects.

THE SAMPLE POPULATION

Tables 4.1, 4.2, and 4.3 show sample rural households in the three counties under review total 358 with 1,625 sample population. Table 5.1 reveals their features in terms of sex, age group, and level of education by virtue of statistics from cross classification of the sample population. Marked statistical results can be summarized as the following three aspects:

1. Nearly 80 percent of the population are under the age of 45. Two-thirds odd of the sample are people at working ages (15-65 years old). These demonstrate that population are young and labor-resource rich.

Table 5.1—Overview on sample population crossly classified in terms of age sex and level of education

Years of Schooling	Sex		Age											Total	
		Under 7		7-15		15-45		45-65		Over 65					
		N	Percent	N	Percent	N	Percent	N	Percent	N	Percent			N	Percent
None	Male	83	32.4	31	12.1	55	21.5	58	22.7	29	11.3			256	100.0
	Female	67	17.2	32	8.2	161	41.4	90	23.1	39	10.1			389	100.0
	Total	150	23.3	63	9.8	216	33.5	148	22.9	68	10.5			645	100.0
0.1 to 3	Male	8	9.8	37	45.1	17	20.7	14	17.1	6	7.3			82	100.0
	Female	3	3.7	33	40.8	38	46.9	7	8.6	0	0.0			81	100.0
	Total	11	6.8	70	42.9	55	33.8	21	12.8	6	3.7			163	100.0
3 to 6	Male	0	0.0	53	27.7	104	54.4	32	16.8	2	1.1			191	100.0
	Female	0	0.0	36	22.6	104	65.4	19	12.0	0	0.0			159	100.0
	Total	0	0.0	89	25.4	208	59.4	51	14.6	2	0.6			350	100.0
More than 6	Male	0	0.0	13	4.2	263	84.3	32	10.2	4	1.3			312	100.0
	Female	0	0.0	10	6.5	142	91.6	3	1.9	0	0.0			155	100.0
	Total	0	0.0	23	5.0	405	86.5	35	7.6	4	0.9			467	100.0
Aggregates of Sample Population	Male	91	10.8	134	15.9	439	52.2	136	16.2	41	4.9			841	100.0
	Female	70	8.9	111	14.2	445	56.8	119	15.1	39	5.0			784	100.0
	Total	161	9.9	245	15.1	884	54.4	255	15.7	80	4.9			1,625	100.0

2. Rate of illiteracy is high. Illiterate people over the age of seven years account for one-third of the total sample. It is worth noting that the illiteracy rate for the age group 7-15 reaches 25.7 percent, 1.3 percentage points more than that of the age group 15-45 (24.4 percent), thus evidencing the aggravating problem of child dropouts in poor areas in recent years. Without taking remedial measures, the quality of the coming generation of the labor force, on the decline, will be unchecked.

3. Generally, the males enjoy a higher level of education than the females in the same age group, which displays the tendency of bias towards males and against females in household decisions for investment in human resources.

Though the above ratios are not completely equivalent to statistical results from the census on macro level, both are identical with one another in reflecting the features of the population. Therefore, the sample population could be considered representative.

COMPARISON BETWEEN PARTICIPANTS AND NONPARTICIPANTS

In the household questionnaire, each family member is asked about the days he (she) is engaged in Yigong-daizhen projects and the income derived from them. There are four types of answer records received from the interviewed in question: (1) both columns are blank; (2) both columns are furnished with answers; (3) days of participation are given without specifying the amount of income; and (4) the amount of income is answered but the days of participation are absent.

Individuals falling into the first category obviously can be identified as nonparticipants, while people belonging to the second through the fourth categories are participants. The third type of answer is normally due to obligatory work contribution and the fourth is explained by the fact that people cannot remember clearly the exact days of work. Calculations based on the above judgment reveal that project participants total 253, amounting

Table 5.2.-Participation of sample households and individuals at the age of 15-65 in Yigong-daizhen projects

	Participating Households		Nonparticipating Households		Total		Participating Households		Nonparticipating Households		Total	
	Number of Households	Percent	Number of Households	Percent	Number of Households	Percent	Number of People	Percent	Number of People	Percent	Number of People	Percent
County 1	58	48.3	62	51.7	120	100.0	91	26.8	249	73.2	340	100.0
Type 1 of villages	19	47.5	21	52.5	40	100.0	42	40.4	62	59.6	104	100.0
Type 2 of villages	39	97.5	1	2.5	40	100.0	49	38.6	78	61.4	126	100.0
Type 3 of villages	0	0	40	100.0	40	100.0	0	0.0	109	100.0	109	100.0
County 2	39	32.5	81	67.5	120	100.0	52	12.2	374	87.8	426	100.0
Type 1 of villages	39	97.5	1	2.5	40	100.0	52	35.4	95	64.6	145	100.0
Type 2 of villages	0	0.0	40	100.0	40	100.0	0	0.0	151	100.0	151	100.0
Type 3 of villages	0	0.0	40	100.0	40	100.0	0	0.0	128	100.0	128	100.0
County 3	64	54.2	54	45.8	118	100.0	110	28.7	274	71.3	384	100.0
Type 1 of villages	19	47.5	21	52.5	40	100.0	42	30.7	95	69.3	137	100.0
Type 2 of villages	26	68.4	12	31.6	38	100.0	42	32.3	88	67.7	130	100.0
Type 3 of villages	19	47.5	21	52.5	40	100.0	26	22.2	91	77.8	117	100.0
Under entire sample	161	45.0	197	55.0	358	100.0	253	28.7	897	71.3	1,150	100.0

to more than one-fifth of the labor force. The household codes of the participants help conclude altogether 161 households take part in the projects, making 45 percent of total sample households (Table 5.2).

Undoubtedly all project participants have the capacity for work, while nonparticipants include the dependent population. In order to disclose the social and economic characteristics of the participants in the comparison, it is of significance that the nonworking population should be excluded from it. From the perspective of statistics at hand, a simple way to distinguish working and nonworking people is to use age as the yardstick. In line with the normal practice in the areas under survey, working ages range from 15 to 65. In the sample, 1,150 people belong to this group. As a matter of fact, some people beyond this age range also take part in production. For example, among the project participants, two are under the age of 15 and three are over 65 (Tables 5.4 and 5.6). However, they only represent 2 percent of all participants, which is a small number after all. So the focus is still on the population from 15-65 years old when conducting statistical analysis of individual features.

In terms of sample households, the participation rates for the three counties under investigation are 48.3 percent, 32.5 percent, and 54.2 percent, respectively (Table 5.2). It is distinct that the figure for County 1 is the lowest and County 3 is highest. Observing types 1 and 2 of sample villages carefully, we find none of their household participation rates are below 47.5 percent. In the first type of village under County 2, the rate reaches as high as 97.5 percent. The causes for the striking differences lie in the fact that the second type of village under County 2 completed its drinking water projects before 1991. Therefore the sample households in the village give "0" as an answer to the public project-related questions, which reduces the share of participating households in the sample. There are about one-half participating households in the reference groups in County 3, thus increasing the weight of participating households in the sample. The case is like this, a reference village in the county diverted the funds for farmland capital construction in Yigong-daizhen plans to building a makeshift road. Some of the

Table 5.3—Comparison between project participating and nonparticipating
households

Type of Household	Number of Households	Scale of Household	Per Capita Cultivated Land	Labor Force/ Number of People in Household	Per Capita Property	Per Capita* Income	Income from Projects
		(people)	(mu)	(0.0)	(yuan)	(yuan)	(yuan)
First county							
Participating	58	4.2	0.7	0.7	1,183	613	15
Nonparticipating	62	4.2	1.2	0.6	958	520	0
First type of villages							
Participating	19	4.0	0.7	0.7	620	456	3
Nonparticipating	21	4.2	1.6	0.6	1,705	667	0
Second type of villages							
Participating	39	4.2	0.7	0.8	1,457	690	22
Nonparticipating	1	7.0	0.5	0.3	1,239	457	0
Third type of villages							
Participating	0	...	...	...	...	...	...
Nonparticipating	40	4.2	1.0	0.7	559	445	0
Second county							
Participating	39	5.2	3.1	0.7	634	366	66
Nonparticipating	81	5.2	4.5	0.7	580	344	0
First type of villages							
Participating	39	5.2	3.1	0.7	634	366	66
Nonparticipating	1	5.0	3.0	0.6	532	66	0
Second type of villages							
Participating	0	...	...	...	...	...	...
Nonparticipating	40	5.3	3.4	0.7	560	377	0
Third type of villages							
Participating	0	...	...	...	...	...	...
Nonparticipating	40	5.0	5.7	0.6	601	318	0
Third county							
Participating	64	4.2	1.2	0.8	2,443	1,100	64
Nonparticipating	54	4.3	1.2	0.8	1,645	695	0
First type of villages							
Participating	19	4.7	1.5	0.7	1,854	1,278	215
Nonparticipating	21	4.3	1.5	0.8	3,115	1,089	0
Second type of villages							
Participating	26	4.0	0.7	0.7	4,264	1,434	0
Nonparticipating	12	4.8	0.8	0.8	1,170	682	0
Third type of villages							
Participating	19	3.9	1.6	0.8	541	463	0
Nonparticipating	21	4.0	1.1	0.7	445	309	0

* Household per capita income here does not include income from projects.

nonparticipating households became participating ones as a result. However, they provided obligatory workdays (see Table 5.3) without pay. In view of the fact that these two cases have no substantial bearing on the present analysis of differences in social and economic conditions between village communities themselves and between rural households, this study will continue to use previous classification of sample villages.

Now a case-by-case review of individual participation rates of each type of sample villages shows that they are all below household participation rates, which is in conformity with the calculation results of the entire sample. It seems that this phenomenon is closely connected with the labor organization method of villages: an equal opportunity is given to every household for participation.

A comparison of major social and economic indicators (Table 5.3) of participating and nonparticipating households helps reveal that two kinds of sample households under the same studied areas have few differences in household size and family labor resources. This generally reflects the similarity of rural household structure in each studied area. In most cases, per capita land of the participating households is less than that of the nonparticipating. Here, the indicators which could figure out land qualities are not available. Therefore, we cannot evaluate wealth of the households merely according to the per capita area of their cultivated land. Moreover, free transfer of land is forbidden by law, then, it is difficult to calculate land value and include the value in statistics for household property. However, judging from per capita property and income indicators for each household in Table 5.3, we find project participating households are normally somewhat richer than nonparticipants. As a result, a conclusion could be made, namely that the projects not only target at the poorest rural households. However, we cannot say with certainty that the projects target only at rich households.

Tables 5.4, 5.5, and 5.6 study social and economic characteristics of individuals. The only economic indicator in these tables is "property situation" so as to show the disparity between the rich and the poor of the sample population. Income indicator is not utilized here because it is a variable with

Table 5.4—Comparison between project participants and nonparticipants
     in County 1 (Linqu/Shandong)

Social and Economic Characteristics	Participants Number of People	Percentage	Nonparticipants (15-65 years old) Number of People	Percentage
Sex				
Male	69	75.8	110	44.2
Female	22	24.2	139	55.8
Total	91	100.0	249	100.0
Age				
<15	1	1.1	...	...
15-45	68	74.7	195	78.3
45-65	21	23.1	54	21.7
>65	1	1.1	...	...
Total	91	100.0	249	100.0
Level of education (years of schooling)				
0	7	7.7	31	12.5
0.1-3	6	6.6	26	10.4
3-6	23	25.3	74	29.7
>6	55	60.4	118	47.4
Total	91	100.0	249	100.0
Property situation[a]				
Poor	29	31.9	74	29.7
Medium	32	35.2	77	30.9
Better-off	30	32.9	98	39.4
Total	91	100.0	249	100.0

[a] The way of classification for property groups is the same as that in Table 5.3.

... = Data not available.

Table 5.5—Comparison between project participants and nonparticipants
in County 2 (Xiji/Ningxia)

Social and Economic Characteristics	Participants		Nonparticipants (15-65 years old)	
	Number of People	Percentage	Number of People	Percentage
Sex				
Male	40	76.9	178	47.6
Female	12	23.1	196	52.4
Total	52	100.0	374	100.0
Age (years)				
<15	0	0.0	...	...
15-45	36	69.2	289	77.3
45-65	16	30.8	85	22.7
>65	0	0.0	...	...
Total	52	100.0	374	100.0
Level of education (years of schooling)				
0 34	65.4	212	56.7	
0.1-3	2	3.9	16	4.3
3-6	6	11.5	69	18.4
>6	10	19.2	77	20.8
Total	52	100.0	374	100.0
Property situation[a]				
Poor	14	26.9	119	31.8
Medium	17	32.7	128	34.2
Better-off	21	40.4	127	34.0
Total	52	100.0	374	100.0

[a] The way of classification for property groups is the same as that in
Table 5.3.

... = Data not available.

Table 5.6—Comparison between project participants and nonparticipants in County 3 (Wangcang/Sichuan)

Social and Economic Characteristics	Participants Number of People	Percentage	Nonparticipants (15-65 years old) Number of People	Percentage
Sex				
Male	64	58.2	122	44.5
Female	46	41.8	152	55.5
Total	110	100.0	274	100.0
Age				
<15	1	0.9	...	...
15-45	79	71.8	217	79.2
45-65	28	25.5	57	20.8
>65	2	1.8	...	...
Total	110	100.0	274	100.0
Level of education (years of schooling)				
0	25	22.7	64	23.4
0.1-3	9	8.2	17	6.2
3-6	24	21.8	63	23.0
>6	52	47.3	130	47.4
Total	110	100.0	274	100.0
Property situation[a]				
Poor	27	24.6	96	35.0
Medium	32	29.1	103	37.6
Better-off	51	46.4	75	27.4
Total	110	100.0	274	100.0

[a] The way of classification for property groups is the same as that in Table 5.3

... = Data not available.

Table 5.7—Project participation rates of different property groups in
counties under survey

Property Group	County 1		County 2		County 3	
	Number of People	Rate of Participation	Number of People	Rate of Participation	Number of People	Rate of Participation
Poor	103	28.2	133	10.5	123	22.0
Medium	109	29.4	145	11.7	135	23.7
Better-off	128	23.4	148	14.2	126	40.5

Notes: Number of people in a property group = participants + nonparticipants (15-65); project
participation rate = (Number of participants in each group/Number of people in the
group) · 100 percent.

much fluctuation as compared with property on the one hand; on the other hand, Yigong-daizhen projects have direct effects on the income level of sample households while their impact on property situation is indirect. Therefore, considering maximized exclusion of these impacts, we consider it is more suitable to use property than income to disclose economic features of the individuals. The steps to divide property groups are: first make a list of rankings from low to high of all sample individuals in accordance with their household per capita property, then divide the sequence into three equal parts, namely three property groups, such as poor, medium, and better-off. On this basis, the frequencies of project participants and nonparticipants from 15-65 are figured out. At last, we can get the composition of property groups for the participants and nonparticipants, respectively.

In County 1, participants roughly have equal representation in all three property groups, namely participants in each group make up around one-third of the total. In Counties 2 and 3, the share of participants from the better-off group gets to more than 40 percent. It appears that the relatively rich in these two counties receive special considerations. In comparing participation rates of each property group based on Tables 5.4, 5.5, and 5.6, we find there is not a great difference (Table 5.7) in project participation rates of various property groups except for the better-off group in County 3. This exactly shows that Yigong-daizhen projects are characteristic of regional targeting mechanisms, which, by no means, excludes the nonpoor. The primary objective in completing these projects serves to improve the infrastructure and social services of poor areas rather than increase employment and income for the poorest.

The demographic features of project participants are embodied in such indicators as sex, age, and level of education (Tables 5.4, 5.5, and 5.6). Undoubtedly male participants are the main force in projects in the three counties. County 3 enjoys the highest rate of female participation—23.4 percent; County 1 occupies a second place—13.7 percent; the last comes County 2—below 6 percent. Of the total participants in each county, women in County 3 account for around two-fifths, while the shares of those in Counties 1 and 2 are both lower than one-fourth. The fact can be interpreted in the following manner: County 3 (Wangcang County/Sichuan Province) is located in South China, while Counties 1 and 2 (Linqu County/Shandong Province and Xiji County/Ningxia Hui Autonomous Region) are situated in northern China. Besides richer family labor resources (number of working people/number of people in the household) in the former, traditionally women in the south take part more extensively in outdoor production than those in the north. In addition, we cannot neglect the fact that County 2 is a region where Hui minority nationality live in compact communities. The religious customs of this nationality comparatively restrict women's participation in outdoor work.

As mentioned earlier, the majority of the sample population are under the age of 45. The age distribution of project participants reflects this demographic feature: more than 70 percent of all participants belong to age group 15-45. Among nonparticipants, 80 percent fit into the same age group. As compared with working population from 45 to 65, this rate has overriding dominance. Though population in developed areas in China have nearly the same age characteristics, an overwhelming majority of young people there are engaged in secondary and tertiary industries, leaving production in primary industry to the old and women. This cannot but arouse our concerns for the serious problem of underemployment for young and robust labor force in poor areas. This exactly forms the basis for village communities to mobilize young and robust manpower to work with Yigong-daizhen projects.

The level of education for sample population is expressed in terms of years of schooling. The distribution of project participants and nonparticipants in groups with different levels of education is similar in each county. Yet disparities between counties are too evident. Consistent with the remarks on levels of education for population in related counties under review in Chapter 3.2, labor force in County 2 (Xiji) shows the highest rate of illiteracy, which is over 56 percent. In contrast to this, nearly half of all laborers in Counties 1 and 3 have received more than six years of education at school. The rate of illiteracy is lowest in County 1, with the figure a bit above 10 percent. In China, the length of schooling for primary schools is six years (in the 1970s, it was changed to five years). Any education fewer than six years is insufficient to equip children with a necessary knowledge of basic Chinese and arithmetic. Using this as a reference to observe the distribution of level of education for laborers, we can infer decisionmaking principles governing human resource investment for rural households: either support children in finishing their primary schooling, or leave them alone and let them become illiterate. No matter what the case is, statistics from Tables 5.4, 5.5, and 5.6 demonstrate that there is still a far cry for poor areas to accomplish universal secondary education. Illiteracy elimination should be the primary human resource investment project for such stark poverty counties as Xiji.

SELECTION OF THE PARTICIPANTS

The description in Chapter 5.2 of the social and economic features of project participants is inadequate to identify factors significantly affecting decisionmaking of individuals to participate in projects. By virtue of Probit Probability Model (Pindyck and Rubinfeld 1992), not only can these factors be pinpointed, individual participation behavior can also be predicted.

In countries like India, Nepal, and Botswana, which have projects similar to Yigong-daizhen, whether or not to participate in projects is determined by individual choices, once the level of payment is decided. As a result, decisionmaking models on participation behavior normally employ social and economic features of individuals as explanatory variables, such as family size, sex of head of household, ages of family members, level of education, and per capita possession of livestock, and so forth (Teklu 1992; Webb 1992). The situation in China is by no means the same.

Participation of households and individuals in Yigong-daizhen projects is mainly dependent on whether the village community they inhabit gets projects instead of their personal wishes. As pointed out in Chapter 4, normal procedures of organizing participants are conducted first by competent authorities at the county level to select project villages with the help of township government. Then village communities assign construction work to households. Which family member takes part in the project eventually fits into the scope of decisionmaking by households themselves. In view of this, probit models are used to estimate the probability of participation in the projects for the villages, households, and individuals, respectively. There are three conclusions that can be drawn from the village-level model (Table 5.8):

1. County and township governments do not necessarily choose the project sites based on whether or not a village established a "system of obligatory labor contribution," but do choose project sites based on village size. The larger the population of a village is, the more likely it is to be involved in projects.

2. Villages with favorable environmental conditions are more likely to get projects. The role of the irrigation index in the model, which indicates conditions for agricultural production in village communities, seems to testify to this point, but it is not statistically significant at the villager level.

3. Villages with more farmland per capita are less likely to get projects, which means that those with more (surplus) labor are supported more.

4. Distances from village to county seat and from village to township have been brought into the model as indices reflecting the relationship between villages and governments. (County seats and townships are places where the governments at the two levels are located.) The results suggest that within counties, the more remote areas get preferential treatment.

In the household-level model (Table 5.9), two village variables, "number of households in a village" and "irrigation index," are included. Because both irrigated and rainfed areas of farmland tend to be distributed among households within a village according to household size, the index can be applied to all households within the same village. The significance of the two variables confirmed the conclusion, derived from Model 1, that participating households are more likely to be located in larger villages. Yet, because the poor make up a larger share of the population in areas where the

projects are carried out and because of the principle of equal opportunity for
participation by all households and laborers enforced by village communities, the results of Model 2 indicated that households that are relatively rich
in labor resources, poor in land, and low in per capita assets value participate more in the projects. While this may be these households' free choice, it
can also be interpreted as a result of the regulated access to participation.

Table 5.8—Estimation of the probability of participation in Yigong-
       daizhen projects by village, Probit Model 1

Variable	Coefficient	t-Ratio
Population	0.31068E-02*	1.838
Distance from village to township	-0.13630	-1.396
Distance from village to county seat	0.25353E-01*	1.860
System of obligatory labor contribution	-0.94305	-0.622
Irrigation index of farmland	4.4919	1.404
Per capita farmland of a village	-1.3306*	-1.836
Constant	0.45017	0.177
N = 34		

* Significant at .10 level.

Table 5.9—Estimation of the probability of participation in Yigong-
       daizhen projects by household, Probit Model 2

Variable	Coefficient	t-Ratio
Per capita farmland of household	-0.17*	-3.30
Irrigation index of farmland	1.71*	4.80
Labor index of household (labor force/household size)	0.44	1.30
Per capita assets	-0.45E-04	-1.05
Number of households in a village	0.21E-02*	3.10
Constant = -0.80		
N = 358		
Cases correctly predicted = 68.4 percent		

* Significant at .01 level.

Table 5.10—Estimation of the probability of individual participation in Yigong-daizhen projects, Probit Model 3

Variable	Coefficient	t-Ratio
Age	0.19E-01**	4.94
Sex (1 = male, 0 = female)	0.47**	4.92
Years of education	0.32E-01*	1.89
Per capita farmland of household	-0.21**	-6.37
Constant = -1.41		
N = 1,145		
Cases correctly predicted = 78.6 percent		

* Significant at .05 level.

** Significant at .01 level.

Probit Model 3 was derived by estimating the probability of individual participation in the projects (Table 5.10). Data for the estimation are based on the records of individual participants and nonparticipants between 15 and 65 years of age—a total of 1,145 people. Several conclusions can be drawn from Model 3 to supplement those drawn from Models 1 and 2.

1. Laborers from households with less land tend to participate more in the projects. This may be because they have lower opportunity costs in agriculture.

2. Male laborers show a higher probability of involvement than females. The reasons for this may be twofold. First, the payments for moving earth and stones are according to task rates that may favor males (due to physical strength). Hence, the active participation of the male laborers can be seen as an efficiency decision by the household. Second, the conventional division of labor between males and females in farmers' families assigns household chores, livestock production, and field work to women, limiting the extent of their participation in projects.

3. Laborers with a higher educational level and older laborers are more inclined to participate.

The analysis suggests that even within poor areas, the criterion for government approval for starting new projects is efficiency—the success of the projects and the effectiveness of the investments. This is consistent with the thinking of the central and provincial governments regarding allocation of resources for the projects: the order of priority among water supply projects is "easy projects first," followed by difficult ones. Emphasis is also placed on the reliability of water sources. Among road construction projects, priority has been given to roads that permit access to resources such as mines and forests and roads that strengthen the existing network. Furthermore, the success or failure of a project serves as an important indicator in assessing the achievements of government officials at the grassroots level. This also explains why township governments usually choose villages with better conditions to be the sites of new projects.

In contrast to this project, village communities have practiced the principle of equality in the recruitment of the labor force for the projects, which means rural households and individuals enjoy equal opportunities in project participation. However, households with lower land and asset base actually turn out to be involved more in the projects compared to the relatively well-to-do people, highlighted by the analysis.

SUMMARY

Statistical analysis of this chapter displays that most of village communities participating in Yigong-daizhen projects are endowed with relatively favorable social and economic conditions in studied counties. It shows that even in poor areas, the base of government's project approval is on the principle of efficiency that ensures the success of projects and effectiveness of investment. This is in conformity with the conceptions of central and provincial governments on project resource allocation. For example, the order of water supply projects is easy ones first followed by difficult ones with stress on reliability of water sources; in road construction projects, priority is given to "resource roads" and "network roads." The success or failure of a project serves as an important indicator to assess the achievement of government officials on a grass-roots level. This also explains why township governments choose villages with better conditions to grant projects.

Different from above practice, the principle of equity is adopted to mobilize and organize labor force by villages: households and individuals enjoy equal opportunity in project participation. Medium and low property groups account for a large share in population, so they get more chances to be involved in projects as compared with relatively well-to-do population.

Moreover, villages and households with comparatively rich labor resource and less farmland have greater probability of project participation. This proves that Yigong-daizhen projects are effective in providing surplus labor with additional employment. Furthermore, the major part of the participants is middle-aged male labor, which implies that the implementation of the projects channels a way for the robust labor to be involved in sectorial labor migration.

6

IMPACT OF THE PROJECTS ON PROPERTY AND INCOME DISTRIBUTION

This chapter, will first of all figure out the income composition of the sample households with a view to identify extra income that the projects generated to the households. Second, decomponent calculation of Gini coefficient helps explain to what extent the projects earnings contribute to income inequality. Third, the method of discriminant analysis is employed to probe into the impact of households' participation in projects on their other economic activities and family welfare. Fourth, the multiple regression serves to identify factors determining household income. Finally, a brief discussion of capital, liabilities, and investment status of rural households will be conducted.

INCOME COMPOSITION OF SAMPLE HOUSEHOLDS

The concept of "disposable income" here follows the definition of "net income of peasant households" provided by the State Statistical Bureau (*The Chinese Yearbook of Statistics* 1991, 307). In 1991, per capita net income of peasant households in China reached 709 yuan. The sample statistics made by the authors show that per capita income of the households in the

Table 6.1—Per capita income structure for average sample household in the first county (Linqu/Shandong) in 1991[a]

Source of Per Capita Income	Type 1 Value (yuan)	Type 1 Percent	Type 2 Value (yuan)	Type 2 Percent	Type 3 Value (yuan)	Type 3 Percent	Sample Aggregate Value (yuan)	Sample Aggregate Percent
Farming incomes	321	59.2	455	66.9	349	77.6	376	67.3
Family nonfarming incomes	91	16.8	6	0.9	21	4.7	39	6.9
Wages	91	16.8	146	21.5	14	3.1	84	15.1
Gathering earnings	0	0.0	0	0.0	14	3.1	5	0.8
Net public transfers[b]	9	1.6	23	3.3	20	4.5	17	3.1
Private transfers	3	0.6	5	0.7	4	0.8	4	0.7
Rental from productive assets	20	3.7	4	0.6	11	2.4	12	2.1
Interests and others	6	1.1	21	3.1	17	3.8	15	2.7
Earnings from public works	1	0.2	20	3.0	0	0.0	7	1.3
Total disposable income[c]	542	100.0	680	100.0	450	100.0	559	100.0

[a] Sample aggregate for the first county includes 120 households, each type of sample is composed of 40 households.

[b] Net income from public transfers equals subsidies and relief funds from government and collective minus taxation and community charges.

[c] Per capita disposable income is the sum total of the nine income components.

Table 6.2—Per capita income structure for average sample household in the second county (Xiji/Ningxia) in 1991[a]

Source of Per Capita Income	Type 1 Value (yuan)	Type 1 Percent	Type 2 Value (yuan)	Type 2 Percent	Type 3 Value (yuan)	Type 3 Percent	Sample Aggregate Value (yuan)	Sample Aggregate Percent
Farming incomes	266	63.9	276	71.5	296	91.4	279	74.2
Family nonfarming incomes	7	1.7	28	7.2	0	0.0	12	3.2
Wages	39	9.3	36	9.4	29	9.1	35	9.2
Gathering earnings	0	0.0	3	0.7	0	0.0	1	0.2
Net public transfers	-4	-0.9	2	0.6	-5	-1.6	-2	-0.5
Private transfers	45	10.8	33	8.5	3	0.9	27	7.2
Rental from productive assets	1	0.2	0	0.0	0	0.0	0	0.1
Interests and others	0	0.0	8	2.1	1	0.2	3	0.8
Earnings from public works	63	15.0	0	0.0	0	0.0	21	5.6
Total disposable income	354	100.0	386	100.0	324	100.0	376	100.0

[a] Sample aggregate for the second county includes 120 households. Each type of sample is composed of 40 households.

Table 6.3-Per capita income structure for average sample household in the third county (Wangcang/Sichuan) in 1991[a]

Source of Per Capita Income	Type 1		Type 2		Type 3		Sample Aggregate	
	Value	Percent	Value	Percent	Value	Percent	Value	Percent
	(yuan)		(yuan)		(yuan)		(yuan)	
Farming incomes	627	48.1	488	42.1	352	88.4	494	51.1
Family nonfarming incomes	218	16.7	340	29.4	0	0.0	188	19.4
Wages	250	19.2	192	16.6	21	5.4	159	16.4
Gathering earnings	49	3.7	0	0.0	0	0.0	18	1.8
Net public transfers	-2	-0.1	33	2.8	1	0.8	10	1.1
Private transfers	20	1.6	54	4.7	16	4.1	30	3.1
Rental from productive assets	7	0.6	33	2.9	0	0.0	13	1.4
Interests and others	21	1.6	17	1.5	5	1.3	14	1.5
Earnings from public works	112	8.6	0	0.0	0	0.0	41	4.2
Total disposable income	1,302	100.0	1,157	100.0	395	100.0	967	100.0

[a] Sample aggregate for the third county is 118 households. The first type includes 40 households; the second type, 38; the third type, 40.

first county (Linqu) is 150 yuan lower than the national average. The figure for households in the second county (Xiji) is about one-half of the national average. Per capita income for the third county (Wangcang) is well above the national figure, topping 967 yuan (Tables 6.1, 6.2, and 6.3).

In view of this, it seems that a conclusion can be made: namely, that the third county no longer falls in the category of poverty counties now. As a matter of fact, a look at the households in the reference group (the third type of villages) will help disclose that their level of income is not very much different from that of the households in the second county. This group of the households represents the mountainous population living above the altitude of 800 meters in the third county (Wangcang). They account for 30 percent of total county population, yet the mountain areas they inhabit cover 65 percent of total county territory. Most of the first and second types of villages are rich localities in the third county, with the former rich in coal and marble resources and the latter located in flatland. Both enjoy either natural endowment or favorable geographic location. Among the sample households in the third county, seven households have per capita income over 1,000 yuan, of which six belong to the first type of villages and one to the second type of villages. They are all characterized by diversified family economic activities such as vegetable-growing, pig-raising, engagement in commerce and transportation or contracting construction projects, and so forth. All these show that diversified economy turns out to be a path leading to better-off for peasant households in poor areas. This diverts our attention to income structure of the households because it serves as an indicator reflecting sources of income for these households.

In order to study the diversified operations of peasant households, income of sample households is broken down into nine components in line with their sources. Of these, agricultural income refers to gross margin the households acquire by way of engaging in cropping production and animal husbandry (namely total value of output minus variable cost, variable cost here excludes expenses from utilization of household labor). Household nonagricultural income is also calculated in accordance with the concept of gross margin (turnover minus variable cost), which actually is resulted from the activities of farmers' family enterprises established in nonagricultural sectors such as processing, handicraft, commerce, and transport. Wages indicate nonagricultural off-farm earnings that family members get. Though these two types of income are both from nonagricultural sources, yet under the former circumstances, the households allocate production factors of all kinds so as to gain income; while, in the second case, individuals only contribute their labor.

Among the income components, agricultural income evidently enjoys the biggest share, thus demonstrating that agriculture still constitutes the most important source of income for peasant households. A comparison of the income structures of the households in the three types of villages helps to reveal the fact that of all the counties under survey, per capita disposable income of an average household in the reference group is lower than that in the two types of project villages with agricultural income occupying a relatively bigger proportion. This means the share of agricultural income declines with the increase of total disposable income and, at present, the rise of income for farmers mainly is dependent upon the success of nonagricultural economic activities (Zhu Ling 1992).

Under most circumstances, the share of nonagricultural income for sample households is lower than the percentage of wages. This shows exactly that the households give rational responses to the availability of their resources: due to capital shortage and manpower surplus, farmers try their best to get income by offering labor service. Tables 6.1, 6.2, and 6.3 display that even in Xiji County, where income is at a fairly low level, farmers provide their families with nearly 10 percent of disposable income in the form of wages. Compared with those in different types of villages, the two kinds of nonagricultural income for average sample household in the reference of villages show the lowest percentages. This indicates that these households encounter much difficulty in accumulating capital and are faced with more obstacles hindering labor mobility.

Foraging mainly hinges on natural conditions households live under; therefore it is an activity undertaken by only a few families. Income from foraging accounts for no more than 4 percent of total household disposable income at most. Net income from public transfers is also an income component with small share. Some households have negative value on this item because the tax they submit coupled with community charges exceeds income transfers they directly get from the state or collectives. The state adopts the policy of tax exemption and reduction to poverty-stricken areas; as a result, the households in these areas do not have to assume heavy tax burden. In 1991, per capita tax submission for sample households ranges from 4 to 9 yuan, while per capita subsidy and relief fund reaches around 20 yuan. It is community charges that make net income from public transfers negative. Sample households annually paid 12 to 37 yuan per capita as community charges.

In areas under study, income from private transfers mostly refers to money or gifts presented among households because of wedding and funeral ceremonies or festival visits. The amount of presents differs in areas with customs. Moreover, the amount of household disposable income also serves as a constraining factor even in a same area with same customs. The share of income from private transfers only forms less than 1 percent of total household income in the first county (Linqu); in the third county (Wangcang), the income at most makes up for no more than 5 percent of the total; while in the second county (Xiji), it is the third largest source of income only after agricultural income and wages, averaging 7.2 percent of the total.

The seventh and eighth income components, namely rents to production assets and interest and others can be summarized as capital returns. The shares of the two components are all below 3 percent, which shows the insignificance of this type of income, at present, to peasant households.

Projects earnings can be regarded as a kind of additional income to the households. Though it originates from a nonagricultural field, this source is quite uncertain. Communities to which the households belong can not possibly get a public construction project year after year. In accordance with the calculation of the data in Table 5.3, about 60 percent of project participation households acquired   projects earnings. The average income from projects for involved households in the first county gets to around 2 to 3 percent of family disposable income. In the second county, the rate is 15.3 percent; in the third one, the number reads 16.8 percent. All these show that projects generated sizable income to participant households in the second and third counties. It is a different case as far as the households in the first county are concerned. The same conclusion can also be drawn by looking at data from Tables 6.1, 6.2, and 6.3. The interpretation of the data can be traced back to Chapter 3.2, in which the authors mentioned that one feature of the economic growth strategy in the first county is to mobilize farmers to take part in infrastructure construction in the form of labor accumulation or, rather, labor tax levy. The strategy requires two preconditions for its implementation: first, the issue of food shortages has been basically resolved; second, farmers accept to this method of public accumulation.

The description in this section can be summed up as follows: income for most households in poor areas is still below national average. In the same area, households successful in engaging in diversified economies record higher income. Yigong-daizhen projects provide participants with no more than 17 percent of extra income at most.

INCOME INEQUALITIES

The descriptive statistics show that of the sample households, only a portion of participants get income from projects. However, up to now, nothing is known about the distribution of project income among households and to what extent the distribution affects the inequality in total disposable income. Decomponent calculation of Gini coefficient will be employed to clarify all these points.

Gini coefficient exposes the magnitude of income inequality. In the process of calculation, per capita household disposable income is used as an income variable in order to remove the influence of different household's size. All individuals from each sample household serve as a corresponding population variable. The distribution of the entire disposable income of the sample households as well as that of each income component are computed in order to show the impact of public work projects on the income distribution. The contribution the distribution of each income component makes to overall Gini coefficient is dependent upon its share in total disposable income, its correlation with the latter, and the extent of its own inequality.

Table 6.4—Income inequality[a] among sample households in the three studied counties, 1991

Source of Per Capita Income	Lingu County (Shandong)			Xiji County (Ningxia)			Wangcang County (Sichuan)		
	Share of Income	Gini Coefficient[b]	Contribution[b] to Overall Gini	Share of Income	Gini Coefficient[b]	Contribution[b] to Overall Gini	Share of Income	Gini Coefficient[b]	Contribution[b] to Overall Gini
	(percent)			(percent)			(percent)		
Farming incomes	67.4	0.264	47.1	74.2	0.270	51.7	51.1	0.268	21.1
Family nonfarming incomes	6.9	0.961	16.4	3.2	0.947	6.6	19.4	0.930	39.8
Wages	15.1	0.767	25.3	9.2	0.836	14.8	16.4	0.776	20.6
Gathering earnings	0.8	0.960	1.0	0.2	0.981	0.6	1.8	0.929	1.6
Net public transfers	3.6	0.876	2.6	0.8	0.967	0.9	1.9	0.929	1.4
Private transfers	0.7	0.927	0.3	7.2	0.904	16.0	1.4	0.788	2.1
Rental from productive assets	2.1	0.974	4.3	0.1	0.992	0.3	3.1	0.788	2.7
Interests and others	2.7	0.825	1.4	0.8	0.986	1.8	1.4	0.986	1.8
Earnings from public works	1.3	0.803	1.6	5.6	0.837	7.3	1.5	0.925	8.9
Total disposable income	100.0[c]	0.304	100.0	100.0[c]	0.331	100.0	100.0[c]	0.437	100.0

[a] Concerning the method of calculation, see Ranis and Kuo (1978) and Fields (1980); on details of calculations, see Zhu Ling and Jiang Zhongyi (1994).

[b] Gini coefficient of each income component as well as that of the total disposable income.

[c] When a component income of a sample household appeared to have a negative value, it would be replaced by zero. Thus, taking the total sample households as a whole, the overall disposable income would be less than the sum of all the component incomes, while the sum of the shares of the nine income components would be a little bigger than 100.0.

Of the three studied counties, the third county experiences the most severe income inequality with sample households having an overall Gini coefficient of 0.437, which is larger than the national one (around 0.33). Income
inequality in the first and second counties is generally at the same level with
their overall Gini coefficients of 0.304 and 0.331, respectively (Table 6.4).
Gini coefficients of project income in all three counties are bigger than their
respective overall Gini coefficients, thus demonstrating that the distribution
of this income component plays the role of aggravating total income inequality. However, this role is insignificant in the first and second counties
and important in the third county: Gini coefficient of the project income in
the latter reaches as high as 0.974, showing serious inequality in distribution: some people with higher income benefit more from project participation. Because of its relatively small share, the projects earnings fail to become the biggest contributing factor to income inequality. The biggest per
capita project earnings of a household in the third county is 3,600 yuan, yet
this record is by no means made by any of the seven households whose per
capita disposable income surpasses 1,000 yuan. Of the seven, only two
families got remuneration from projects with per capita earnings of 24 and
37 yuan separately, which are both lower than the county average (Table
6.3). The household that received highest pay from projects is one lorry
owner specializing in transportation. His earnings from projects actually
includes capital returns.

According to the above comparison, it could be thought that the authorities in charge of projects in the third county not only adopt the principle of
efficiency in selecting project sites, but also fail to pay due attention to equity in organizing the construction work. They may tend to contract some
work of the projects to people with capital-intensive technology. By so doing, the difficulties in project organization have obviously been minimized.
But the consequences are as follows: most of the households participating in
projects get a limited amount of income, while a few comparatively well-to-
do households who possess capital necessary for construction work benefit
the most. This tendency is even more evident in the way of organizing the
construction of terraced fields and reservoir in the second county
(Xiji/Ningxia). It is worth noting that even when the labor force in the

county is experiencing a surplus, competent authorities there purchase over 10 tractors and organize a specialized team to construct terraced fields so as to create employment opportunities and income for the team that is under their direct jurisdiction. This undoubtedly weakens the poverty alleviation purpose of Yigong-daizhen projects. Because these projects began to be executed in 1992, they do not fall into the scope of author's survey sample and the impact of this form of organization on the distribution of project earnings is not to be covered in Table 6.4.

All Gini coefficients for agricultural income in the three counties are smaller than their respective overall Gini coefficients, thus indicating the former helps reduce income inequality. However, due to the big share of agricultural income, it still serves as the number one or two contributing element to total inequality. Existing studies home and abroad have testified that the concentration of land ownership constitutes the most important factor to inequality in agricultural income. Agricultural workers without land more often than not are reduced to lowest income group. The present land tenure system in rural China prevents it from occurring. The principle of equal allocation of land within the same community and state regulations prohibiting free sales and purchase of land may hinder the factor mobilities and adversely affect the allocation efficiency of arable land. Yet building on the basis, they guarantee the basic food requirement of rural population and keep inequality in agricultural income at a low level. The statistical analyses in this section have proved this point. Even in the third county, where income inequality is most severe, Gini coefficient for agricultural income is only at around 0.2.

The dependence of peasant households in the same area on natural environment and market condition at the local gives them similar structure of agricultural production. Take the proportion of income from cropping production to total agricultural income for average household in the three types of villages as an example: the biggest difference in those shares for households in the same county is not over 14 percentage points: the percentage for the first county ranges from 65.7 percent to 79.1 percent; the second county, 91.8 percent to 99.7 percent; the third county, 81.2 percent to 86.1 percent. In addition, the extension pattern of agricultural technology from central to local and grass-roots level results in the fact that the households in same area normally apply similar technology. All these factors contribute to equal distribution of agricultural income.

The Gini coefficients for family nonagricultural income and wages are both above 0.7, showing great inequality in their distribution among the sample households. Both relative correlation coefficients of these two income components to total income are larger than 0.6, which indicates that households with higher total income acquire more family nonagricultural income and wages. The Gini coefficients of these two income components are bigger than the overall Gini coefficient. This demonstrates that they help widen income inequality. Though the share of the two components is smaller than that of agricultural income, their contribution to overall income inequality is quite significant. In the third county, in particular, their combined contribution accounts for more than 60 percent. Therefore, we can conclude that under circumstances when distribution of agricultural income is generally equal, distribution of nonagricultural income has a decisive bearing on overall inequality.

The apparent inequality in the distribution of these two kinds of nonagricultural income is mainly attributable to the differences in getting capital and employment opportunities by peasant households in nonagricultural fields. The rapid development of rural nonagricultural sectors is a product of economic reforms in the 1980s. They represent completely new and unfamiliar fields to most farmers in poor areas. Whether individual farmers enter the fields and achieve success will be dependent upon their talent, enterprising spirit, information on hand, and family economic capacity. Meanwhile, local infrastructure, capital accumulation, and market maturity serve as constraints. All these determine that households engaged in family nonagricultural entrepreneurial activities are those small number of pioneers; it is not common that farmers here can work as nonagricultural wage earners. Of course, it is not as difficult to earn wages from nonagricultural fields as to get family enterprise income after all. So distribution of wages is more equal than that of households' nonagricultural income with a Gini coefficient of 0.5.

Of the other income components that make relatively small contribution to overall Gini coefficient, it is worth noting the distribution of net public transfers. It has high Gini coefficient and low relative correlation coefficient, meaning people with lower income enjoy more net public transfers and with higher income receive less. Obviously it reduces inequality in the distribution of total income.

In sum, agriculture constitutes the major income source for sample households. It is nearly equally distributed among households. In comparison, nonagricultural income has a high degree of inequality. Distribution of projects earnings exacerbates inequality in total disposable income. Yet, due to its small share, its influence is quite limited.

RELATION BETWEEN PROJECTS AND FAMILY WELFARE

The above discussion of rural household income from projects has not directly taken into consideration the farmers' opportunity costs for their involvement. To obtain information on this, the survey included some related direct questions to farmers.

Table 6.5 reports the responses to these questions in interviews with households. Several conclusions can be drawn. First, for most of the laborers (78.1 percent), their participation in the projects resulted in a decrease in their leisure time. Because Yigong-daizhen projects were usually carried out during the slack season in farming, the opportunity cost of their participation in the projects was almost zero (the "leisure time" in this season was not the choice of farmers themselves but a manifestation of idleness of the labor force). This fact constitutes the rationale for low payment and the mobilization of obligatory labor contribution commonly practiced in the construction works.

Second, the working hours of women in almost one-half of the households were increased—in other words, their leisure time was reduced in order to meet the time requirements of agricultural production while male laborers participated in the projects. The rural households made labor inputs by adjusting the deployment of the family labor force. In 54.2 percent of the

Table 6.5—Impact of participation in Yigong-daizhen projects on household work time and children's dislocation

Reaction from Interviewees	Question				
	Stopped Some Other Work (1)[a]	Women Work More (2)[b]	Children Work More (3)[c]	Child at Workplace (Women) (4)[d]	Child at Workplace (Men) (5)[e]
			(percent)		
Yes	21.9	45.8	6.5	6.5	2.0
No	78.1	54.2	93.5	93.5	98.0

[a] Is there any laborer in your family who has stopped other production work to take part in the project?

[b] Have the female members in your family increased their working time in farming due to the participation of male laborers in the projects?

[c] Have the children in your family under 16 years of age increased their working time in domestic labor due to the participation of their parents in the projects?

[d] Do the female members of your family bring with them the children under 16 years old when attending project work?

[e] Do male laborers in your family bring with them the children under 16 years old when attending project work?

Note: A total of 201 households answered these questions, representing 56 percent of the total sample. Among them, 40 households have possibly participated in the projects. But due to their failure to answer questions concerning the number of days of their participation and their earnings from the projects, they were not included.

rural households, participation in projects did not affect the amount of time worked by female laborers, perhaps because these households had more working members or because the timing of the construction work and the slack season in farming coincided.

Third, it was probably because of the abundant labor supply that the impact of farmer participation in the project on children's work (question 3) and children's dislocation from home (questions 4 and 5) was small.

The implementation of projects increases employment and income of participants during that year. This is the short-term effect of projects on income of peasant households or we call it the first round impact. Farmers make investment in fixed assets by using part of projects earnings or purchase additional inputs for production, which may lead to further increase in income. This is regarded as the second round impact (von Braun, Teklu, and Webb 1991). Meanwhile, the completion of projects improves community infrastructure and creates favorable conditions for the households to enjoy future incremental income, which is the long-term role projects can play.

With regard to the disposal of earnings from projects, the overseas scholars engaging in poverty studies express their concerns over the following questions: who is in charge of family income, man or wife? To which portion of income (for instance, income from cash crops or grain crops) man or wife has the disposal right respectively? The interest in these questions originates from the fact that in some South Asian and African countries, man and wife of a family control their portion of family income separately and have respective "sphere of influence." Men and women have different preferences with respect to how to spend their income. Their respective decisions have a remarkable different influence on the family welfare. For instance, when paying visits to Bangarlore area in India, the authors learned that women would normally use income from public works to purchase foodstuffs, which is conducive to improving the nutritional conditions of family members, children in particular, while men would first of all use the money to satisfy their hankering for alcohol. In this case, if the objective of projects aims at upgrading the nutritional standards of the poor, the program should be designed to include women's active participation.

Rural Chinese households normally have unified family financial management. Income earned by individual family members all goes into the family coffer. No matter who takes charge of the family income, man and wife would consult each other when exercising right to income disposal. To a greater or lesser extent, the practice rectifies some of the consumption preferences because of sex difference, which have been confirmed by the authors' sample statistics. The cases that family income managed by male head accounted for 72.5 percent of the project participation households. Women control the family coffer in 9.9 percent of the households. Man and wife jointly manage family finances in the rest of the households. However, the pattern of income disposable by project participants does not significantly correlate with the sex of people. The above percentages only imply that male laborers occupy a dominant position in the family economy.

In order to explore the second round of impact projects have on household income, the authors inquired about project income disposal from involved households by asking questions with multiple choices. Only 3.8 percent of them spent most of the income from projects on procuring draught animals, agricultural machinery, and transport facilities. Less than 1 percent invested the earnings in housing construction. Twenty-one percent of the households bought other input goods, 58.1 percent purchase consumer goods for daily use, and the rest (16.1 percent) have other utilizations.

All in all, about one-fourth of the households put project earnings in the field of production, while most of them decided to improve consumption. Yet no one puts the money in bank. On one hand, farmers get industrial coupons rather than currency as payment. The former cannot be deposited as savings. On the other hand, most of the participants are poor, whose basic necessities have yet to be fully satisfied. Therefore, they are inclined to spend the additional earnings on consumption improvement.

The information mastered by the authors at present is insufficient to evaluate directly the long-term effects projects brought about to the households. Therefore, some intermediate variables will be employed to make a rough judgment about the direction of the influence projects exert. Though the infrastructure in the first and second types of villages might be superior to that in nonproject villages before the project implemented, yet it is for sure that their infrastructure experiences further improvement owing to the construction of road and drinking water facilities. Such improvement accelerates labor mobility and the development of nonfarming sectors and provides convenience for households to adopt advanced technology and inputs in agriculture, which is bound to raise income of the households. Based on this, the authors assume that project and nonproject villages have distinguished differences in the above aspects. Discriminant analysis will be used to testify the assumption.

First of all, four variables that have significant contribution to distinguishing three types of sample villages are figured out through the method of stepwise selection of variables: namely, amount of fertilizers used, percentage of seeded areas with improved varieties, share of nonfarming income, and provision of social services at village level. The first three variables come from the data of sample households. The first variable refers to the actual amount of fertilizer application; the second variable stands for the portion of area with improved varieties to sown area of all major grain crops; the third variable is calculated as (family nonfarming income + wages)/disposable income, which does not include income from projects; the fourth variable is expressed in grades decided in line with the level of social service provision by sample villages (Chapter 4.2). The households in the same village are granted a same mark.

The second step of analysis is to carry out multiple significance test on discriminant effects to the three types of sample villages. The results of calculation are as follows:

Selection Step	Number of Variables in	Wilks' Lambda	Prob < Lambda
1	1	0.4166	0.0001
2	2	0.3998	0.0001
3	3	0.3878	0.0001
4	4	0.3812	0.0001

The results of the last step of selection shows that Wilks' Lambda = 0.3812, p<0.0001, indicating that discriminant function set up with the above four variables has highly significant discriminant effects. On this basis, these four variables are given further general discriminant analysis and squared distances among three types are figured out:

	Generalized Squared Distances to Type		
From Type	1	2	3
1	6.6093	8.7862	11.9329
2	8.0470	7.7351	15.5598
3	12.7215	17.8933	5.9792

The calculation transmits a piece of information worthy of our attention: distance between the first and second types is shortest, while distances from the first and the second to the third type are relatively long. This implies that differences in infrastructure, activities in nonagricultural sectors, and modern agricultural technology application between project villages and non-project villages are far more striking than those in the same aspects between different project villages.

From the calculation, we get a quadratic discriminant function, then the calculation formula for posterior probability (Hartung and Elpelt 1986). The fourth step of analysis is to substitute original observations in the formula of posterior probability and conduct discrimination on each sample household in line with the biggest posterior probability. The new classification of households by way of discrimination is not in complete conformity with the original types:

	Number of Observations into Type			
From Type	1	2	3	Sum
1	73	34	13	120
2	22	84	10	116
3	19	1	100	120
Sum	114	119	123	356*

* There were two missing values in the computation.

If only considering classification of households between project and non-project villages, we will note that only 12 percent of sample households show difference between discrimination results and their real situation. So classification of households in light of projects' coverage of communities can duly reflect the differences among most households. Households discriminated as the third type actually consist of 13 from the first type of villages and 10 from the second type of villages. While of those households living in the third type of villages, 20 are considered to be the first (19) and second (1) types. Descriptive statistics from Chapter 6.1 reveal that average income for the households in project villages is higher than that in nonproject villages. If we look closely at the income level of the special cases, we find that of 23 households which are discriminated from project type of villages to nonproject type of villages, more than one-half have per capita income below 380 yuan, which belong to the lower-income group in project villages. In contrast, with regard to 75 percent of those households living in nonproject villages but discriminated as in project villages, per capita income of their families is over 400 yuan, which is regarded as households with middle or high level of income in their villages. All these show that improvement of infrastructure provides a prerequisite for farmers to enjoy income increase, yet it is not sufficient. Not all households living in the same village can utilize the same favorable infrastructure to develop their family economy.

Discussions in this section confirms that Yigong-daizhen projects is playing and will play a positive role in helping farmers raise their current and future income. As projects progress, participants themselves and their families have never suffered substantial losses in terms of their welfare.

DETERMINANTS OF INCOME

The execution of projects also improves infrastructure and social services in the villages, creating conditions for future increases in rural households' incomes. This is a long-term effect of the projects, which shall be assessed in the context of other income-determining factors. Village infrastructure was assessed on the basis of six factors: accessibility of the village by road (conditioned by being accessible by truck); the existence of supply stations for input materials (improved varieties of crops, chemical fertilizer, and other farm chemicals); and the availability of electricity, medical services, drinking water supply centers, and village primary schools. To obtain an aggregate impression, each factor was assigned one point. Villages with all of the above six kinds of infrastructural conditions and services obviously got six pints. The project villages among the sample generally got more than four points each, while the villages in the reference groups got around 2.5 points each, on average. There are, of course, correlations among these infrastructural conditions (Ahmed and Hossain 1990).

Studies in the past have indicated that income disparities among rural households are generally determined by differences in land ownership or access, capital, labor force, application of modern techniques and input materials in farming activities, as well as infrastructural conditions. A multiple regression analysis below has included indicators that represent the above-mentioned factors— including the household per capita area of cultivated land, the ratio of area under improved varieties to total cultivated land, the irrigation index, household per capita fixed assets, the family labor resource index (labor force/household size), and the educational level of the household head, as independent variables; the dependent variable is household per capita disposable income. The results show the significance of per capita assets of rural households, infrastructural conditions of village communities, chemical fertilizers applied per mu, and the counties with which sample households are affiliated (as dummy variables) to capture other regional influences. The regression model is as follows:

$$I = 121.23 + 0.11 \text{ PCASSET} + 50.59 \text{ PCLAND} + 0.79 \text{ PMFERTI} +$$
$$\quad (-0.885) \qquad (7.848)** \qquad\quad (2.191)* \qquad\quad (3.191)**$$

$$49.14 \text{ INFRA} + 162.11 \text{ COUNTY1} + 350.54 \text{ COUNTY3} +$$
$$\quad (2.253)* \qquad\quad (1.573) \qquad\qquad\quad (3.416)**$$

$$47.59 \text{ IMR}$$
$$\quad (1.244)$$

$$R^2 = 0.365, F (7,350) - 28.777, N = 358.$$

Numbers in parentheses indicate t-ratios.

The signs ** and * indicate significance at the 99- and 95-percent confidence level, respectively.

Variables are

    I = household per capita disposable income

    PCASSET = per capita assets (excluding land)

    PCLAND = per capita cultivated land

    PMFERTI = chemical fertilizer applied per mu

    INFRA = points for infrastructural conditions of village communities in which the sample households live

    COUNTY1 = Linqu County of Shandong Province

    COUNTY3 = Wangcang County of Sichuan Province

    IMR = inverse mills ratio for correcting sample selection bias (Doldon and Makepeace 1987).

The results concerning the dummy variables COUNTY1 and COUNTY3 in the model mean that the incomes of households in Linqu and Wangcang Counties are generally higher than those in Xiji County. The results also imply that, apart from socioeconomic conditions, regional differences in features of the natural environment, such as topography and climate, decisively affect the household income. (Xiji is an extremely dry area, Linqu is located in a sub-dry region, while Wangcang has a mild climate, humid and warm, favorable for agriculture.) The regression results support the hypothesis the improved village infrastructure enhances household income.

The amount of farmland and the use of chemical fertilizers proved to be significant determinants of household income. Moreover, assets stand out as an important factor that determines income differences among households. This variable includes capital goods, housing, and durable consumer goods, but excludes land, because the land market is nonexistent under the present legislation and there are no prices for farmland cultivated by farmers in China.

Household assets are the deposits of incomes earned in the past, and represent the outcome of past economic activity. Therefore, assets not only indicate property amounts, but also farmers' knowledge, skills, and entrepre-

neurship. The latter items are difficult to measure, but they indicate the
quality of human resources that can be mobilized for economic activities.

In the income regression equation, several independent variables
(excluding two dummy variables) that are significant demonstrate—from
different angles—that capital is the most important income determinant.
These variables are "village infrastructure," which results from public investment; "assets"; and "fertilizer application," which not only represents
material input in agriculture, but also the amount of circulating capital
available to rural households. Often, funds allocated for fertilizer procure-
ment make up the largest share of circulating capital for agricultural production in farm households. In view of the fact that indicators representing
asset value all have a positive correlation with income, it is likely that increases in capital possessed by rural households will promote income
growth.

PROPERTY, DEBT, AND INVESTMENT OF SAMPLE HOUSEHOLDS

How could farmers expand there own capital? Relations among earnings
from Yigong-daizhen projects, savings, debts, investment in the survey year,
and the value of fixed assets are examined.

At the survey year, asset distribution is even more unequal than income
distribution. Gini coefficients for household per capita asset in the three
counties under the survey read 0.4232, 0.3555, and 0.5669, respectively.
Here we use "gross asset value" for the calculation on assets distribution;
namely liabilities is not deducted from the sum of fixed assets and savings.
The reason behind it is that most well-to-do households borrow more
money. Sample households are divided into poor, middle, and well-to-do
property groups (Tables 6.6, 6.7, and 6.8) in line with per capita fixed assets so as to show their assets and liabilities. Assets are divided into three
types: productive, nonproductive fixed assets, and financial assets (savings).
In real economic activities, there is no clear distinction between the uses of
certain assets. For example, farmers sometimes utilize bicycles as a means
of transport to engage in county fair trade; sewing machines serve as

Table 6.6—Per capita assets and liabilities of sample households in the first county (Linqu) in 1991[a]

Items	Poor Group	Middle Income Group	Well-to-do Group	Sample Aggregate
Productive fixed assets (yuan)	171	332	1,006	503
Livestock and poultry (percent)	27.6	20.6	8.7	17.6
Large and medium-sized farm tools (percent)	40.6	53.6	39.1	44.4
Machinery for agriculture (percent)	12.5	14.8	8.0	11.4
Machinery for industry (percent)	0.0	0.0	6.4	2.6
Machinery for transport (percent)	0.0	0.0	8.7	3.5
Building for production (percent)	8.7	9.5	27.7	16.7
Others (percent)	10.6	1.5	1.4	3.8
Nonproductive fixed assets (yuan)	1,258	3,166	7,441	3,955
Bicycles, sewing machines (percent)	15.1	8.4	4.6	9.4
Televisions, recorders (percent)	3.5	8.6	5.0	5.7
Housing (percent)	81.4	83.0	90.4	84.9
Total savings at year's end (yuan)	33	144	528	235
Total liabilities at year's end (yuan)	260	361	178	266
Net assets[b] (yuan)	280	723	2012	1005

[a] Because there lacks land market, Tables 6.6, 6.7, and 6.8 do not include the value of land.

[b] Net assets = productive fixed assets + nonproductive fixed assets + total savings at year's end − total liabilities at year's end.

Table 6.7—Per capita assets and liabilities of sample households in the second county (Xiji) in 1991

Items	Poor Group	Middle Income Group	Well-to-do Group	Sample Aggregate
Productive fixed assets (yuan)	561	708	2,873	1,502
Livestock and poultry (percent)	60.0	65.5	48.1	57.8
Large and medium-sized farm tools (percent)	0.0	0.0	1.0	0.3
Machinery for agriculture (percent)	0.0	1.9	18.1	6.8
Machinery for industry (percent)	0.0	0.0	7.1	2.4
Machinery for transport (percent)	0.0	0.2	0.0	0.1
Building for production (percent)	15.6	14.2	17.5	15.8
Others (percent)	24.4	18.2	8.2	16.8
Nonproductive fixed assets (yuan)	767	1,481	2,921	1,723
Bicycles, sewing machines (percent)	12.9	14.1	12.6	13.2
Televisions, recorders (percent)	3.9	4.3	8.7	5.6
Housing (percent)	83.2	81.6	78.7	81.2
Total savings at year's end (yuan)	0	21	10	10
Total liabilities at year's end (yuan)	559	565	471	532
Net assets (yuan)	128	377	950	485

Table 6.8—Per capita assets and liabilities of sample households in the third county (Wangcang) in 1991

Items	Poor Group	Middle Income Group	Well-to-do Group	Sample Aggregate
Productive fixed assets (yuan)	596	837	5,124	2,189
Livestock and poultry (percent)	77.5	62.1	36.1	58.8
Large and medium-sized farm tools (percent)	2.7	20.7	16.3	13.1
Machinery for agriculture (percent)	0.0	0.0	0.0	0.0
Machinery for industry (percent)	0.0	0.0	3.2	1.1
Machinery for transport (percent)	0.0	3.2	18.4	7.1
Building for production (percent)	9.0	13.0	26.0	15.9
Others (percent)	10.8	1.0	0.0	4.0
Nonproductive fixed assets (yuan)	1,442	4,384	13,384	6,413
Bicycles, sewing machines (percent)	0.4	2.3	3.3	2.0
Televisions, recorders (percent)	0.0	3.7	8.7	4.2
Housing (percent)	99.6	94.0	88.0	93.8
Total savings at year's end (yuan)	15	170	1,566	585
Total liabilities at year's end (yuan)	181	161	1,356	567
Net assets (yuan)	403	1,079	4,138	1,875

equipment in family handicraft; living houses sometimes are used for storage and other indoor production activities. Owing to the above reasons,
these items are not excluded in the income analysis.

In fixed assets for productive purposes, livestock and poultry, large and
medium-sized farm implements, and houses for productive purposes are
major components. The share of agricultural transport machinery only
reaches around 18 percent in the well-to-do group. Farmers normally do not
distinguish clearly between these two types of machinery. For instance,
tractors are usually used for transportation. However, how we classify the
machinery does not affect the understanding about this fact: farm produce
processing and transportation are two nonfarm industries that witness the
most rapid development in areas under study, with the development of
transportation going hand in hand with improvement of road conditions.
From this perspective, we can see that road construction projects indirectly
promote capital formation and farmers' income rise.

The value of nonproductive fixed assets is larger than productive fixed
assets, with housing occupying the biggest share in the former. This composition reflects the subsistence economy of farmers characterized by small-
scale production and primitive implements. In addition, compared with productive fixed assets, private ownership of farmers' housing over the past
four decades remained unchanged. Besides requirements for shelter, this
social cause facilitates farmers' preference for investment in housing. Even
well-to-do families give it priority over investment in production (Zhu Ling
1991).

The percentage of savings in rural household assets is lower than 6 percent, which is the smallest asset component. This not only stands for poverty, but also is a manifestation of shortage in liquid capital. Quite a portion
of farmers said, when they were asked questions, that they were worried
about inadequacy of funds instead of that of food. This tendency is also reflected in the expectations of Yigong-daizhen project participants with regard to the form of project payments: 85.6 percent of the households want
cash.

Where does the capital for investment in fixed assets come from, besides
savings? Income from projects by no means serves as the major source of

investment for rural households: less than 4 percent of project participants invested their projects' earnings in fixed assets, while the majority spent the earnings on consumer goods. Loans are the source of capital for investments.

There are two types of loan providers: official financial institutions and individuals, most of whom are relatives and friends of farmers. Annual interest rate of credits from the former ranges from 0.78 percent to 1.1 percent, while the latter does not require interest in the form of currency. Of 96 households getting official loans, 75 percent of them use the loans for investment in production; 14.6 percent use the money for illness treatment; the rest for housing construction and funerals. The order of use with respect to private loans is different (households borrowing money = 155): treatment of illness ranks the first (34.8 percent), followed by investment in production (31.6 percent); housing construction is the third largest use (16.1 percent); weddings and funerals (7 percent) comes out as the fourth; the rest borrows money to purchase commodities for daily use. All of these show that official loans are mainly used for productive investment. Private loans meanwhile are used to cope with major events in everyday life or emergencies.

During the period of the People's Commune (before 1979), the poorer rural households were, the heavier their debt burden became (Zhou Binbin 1991). Since the reforms, that is no longer the case. After the system of absolute egalitarianism was abolished, the ability to repay loans became an important criterion in rural household's eligibility for loans. A situation common in rural areas throughout the world emerged: the poor cannot easily acquire loans. Those who can are normally the nonpoor. In the sample, the correlation coefficient of loans and assets reaches as high as 0.5885. It is worth mentioning that the formation of private assets of rural households has no strong connection to projects earnings; rather, credit plays a determining role. The policy implication of this conclusion is that only when Yigong-daizhen projects are coupled with effective development of rural financial systems can these projects increase the future income of poverty-stricken households.

CONCLUSION AND ITS POLICY IMPLICATION

The following points are proved by means of analytical statistics in this chapter:

1. Income level for overwhelming majority of rural households in poor areas is lower than national average. Yigong-daizhen projects to varying degrees improved income for participants and enabled them to have purchased more consumer goods and input materials. At most, projects' earnings compose one-sixth of disposable income for rural households. Besides, community infrastructure and conditions of social services are upgraded through the projects, which facilitates further income growth of rural households.

2. Normally projects are implemented during slack seasons when a considerable portion of farmers are in a state of involuntary unemployment. Project participation does not bring about any substantial loss to participants themselves and their families.

3. There already exist striking income disparities among rural households in poor areas, which is resulted from inequality in income distribution in nonfarm fields. Some male laborers with comparatively higher level of education and who are young earn wages other than income from farming through spatial and sectoral migration. Those rural households that have set up family nonfarming enterprises and enjoy success not only get increased labor returns due to improved utilization efficiency of labor resources, but also make enterprise profits because of productive investment. Similarly, opportunities of farmers' participation in projects are restricted by amount of project resources, implementation sites, and community barriers. Not all laborers can get this income. As far as participants are concerned, some join in projects together with their machines. So their income from projects is by no means wages only. It also includes capital returns. This causes higher level of inequality in distribution of projects earnings and enlarges overall Gini coefficient. Because of the small share of project income in total disposable income, this influence is quite limited.

4. Income disparities among rural households are caused, first of all, by regional differences. In a same area, community infrastructure, scale of arable land households possess, and material and human capital become determinants of income. Meanwhile, capital formation is mainly dependent on loans.

The above conclusions imply that Yigong-daizhen projects increase income for rural households during the implementation year and welfare as well. Therefore, at present, it is still necessary to continue with such project implementation in poor areas. Yet, the way of project organization leaves much room for improvement. The focus is on helping poor households overcome community barriers and improving their chances of involvement by facilitating labor mobility so as to reduce the extent of income inequality. However, Yigong-daizhen projects only provide an essential condition for households to enjoy long-term income growth. Regional policies and household credit projects should also serve as supportive measures. Only by way of improving the conditions for social and economic development in poor areas and promoting the expansion of private assets of rural households can the objective of gradual and steady poverty alleviation be materialized.

7

FOOD CONSUMPTION AND NUTRITION OF SAMPLE HOUSEHOLDS

T he primary objective of some South Asian and African countries to implement public projects normally serves to create employment opportunities and income for the poor so as to improve their status of food consumption and nutrition, because agricultural workers and small farmers lose their food security during seasonal unemployment period. In China, food security for agricultural population is materialized by virtue of equal land allocation system, operations of official grain supply and marketing agencies in regulating shortages and surpluses and the relief function of civil affairs administration. Against such background, it is not difficult to understand that, among the various Yigong-daizhen projects, the construction of terraced fields has the most direct impact on strengthening the food security of the poor. The road building and drinking water projects are not designed to solve food shortages directly, but to improve infrastructures and social services. However, the projects do have impacts on rural household expenditures, including those for food consumption, through increases in farmers' incomes. This chapter aims to explore the determinants of the consumption expenditures of sample households. This chapter also contains an analysis of the food consumption and nutritional status of the sample population and some insights relevant to policy in this area.

CONSUMPTION EXPENDITURES

The per capita consumption expenditure of the sample households of the three investigated counties was 426, 402, and 825 yuan, respectively. The share of food consumption expenses was 66.3 percent, 64.6 percent, and 67.1 percent, respectively, indicating that differences in the composition of expenditure among the three sample counties were not significant and that the conditions described by Engel's Law were not fully met. Engel's Law may not apply to populations that have not yet stepped over the threshold of poverty. Only when basic requirements for food consumption have been met does the share of food consumption expenses gradually decline as family incomes increase.

The food consumption of rural families is still strongly tied to self-production on the farm. The share of self-produced foods in the total food expenditures of sample households in the three counties was 69.5 percent, 87.6 percent, and 90.4 percent, respectively. It seems that rural household in-cash consumption expenditures are mainly for nonfood consumer goods and service payments (Table 7.1).

Medicine is listed as a separate item when discussing consumption composition because serious illness normally plunges individual rural families into poverty. The fact that poorer households ask more for medicine should be telling enough for decisionmakers to put more emphasis on establishing a medical insurance system in rural areas. Though the cooperative medical system practiced during the People's Commune to some extent contributed to the prevention and treatment of some common diseases, it was far from sufficient to help cure serious sickness. Farmers' families always have to face all by themselves the blow of sudden expense increase and manpower reduction caused by serious illness. Borrowing and relief can only have a cushioning effect.

Cigarettes and wine are popular consumer goods for men in the areas under study. Though they do more harm than good to people's health, they serve as medium of social contact in countryside, where cultural life is lacking. So, the authors put cigarettes and wine consumption and presents in

Table 7.1—Structure of annual per capita consumption expenses for sample households,[a] China, 1991

Items of Expenses		Lingu County			Xiji County			Wangcang County		
		Poor	Middle	Well-to-do	Poor	Middle	Well-to-do	Poor	Middle	Well-to-do
Food	(yuan)	224	286	339	195	259	320	374	596	678
	(percent)	66.2	66.4	66.2	68.0	67.9	60.5	70.0	70.7	62.9
of which:										
Self-provision	(yuan)	138	216	235	165	225	287	350	565	576
Food = 100 percent		61.6	75.5	69.3	84.6	86.9	89.7	93.6	94.8	85.0
Medical care	(yuan)	20	29	24	42	51	71	58	27	42
	(percent)	6.1	6.8	4.6	14.7	13.5	13.5	10.8	3.3	3.9
Cigarettes, wine, and presents	(yuan)	28	34	39	15	19	65	48	83	157
	(percent)	8.4	7.9	7.7	5.2	4.9	12.2	9.0	9.9	14.6
Other	(yuan)	65	82	110	35	52	73	54	136	200
	(percent)	19.3	18.9	21.5	12.1	13.7	13.8	10.2	16.1	18.6
Total	(yuan)	337	431	512	287	381	529	534	842	1,077
	(percent)	100.0	100.0	100.0	100.0	100.0	100.0	100.0	100.0	100.0

[a] Sample households are divided into tercile groups according to household per capita assets.

the same category. The former includes the part for self-consumption, while the latter purely refers to money and goods presented as gifts to others. Among rural households, present from one means income for another. The total value of exchange is almost equal. It is worth noting that the value of present consumption is higher than any other nonfood necessities, which reflects a special economic and cultural phenomenon: under circumstances of lacking social security, people build up intensified relationship with relatives and friends out of their own accord and form safeguard networks by way of personal ties. For instance, when a family falls prey to mishap, farmers usually think of borrowing from relatives and friends. The uses of private borrowing discussed in Chapter 6.5 testify to the point.

The fourth item in Table 7.1 is the sum of all daily necessities and service other than food and medical care expenses, which include clothing, fuel, electricity fee, transportation and postage expenses, and tuition for children, and so forth. Generally speaking, the share of this type of consumption for well-to-do families is larger than poor ones, because, in comparison with the latter, they still have additional payment capacity to procure other consumer goods and services after their basic need for food is satisfied.

FAMILY NUTRITION STATUS

In China, nutrition studies have always been the job of medical scientists and nutritionists, while economists seldom involve themselves in this field. As a result, up to now, research work on nutrition wants analysis and interpretation from social and economic perspectives. Yet, nutrition status is an important indicator in evaluating quality of people's life. Improving the quality of life right serves as the objective and outcome of development. Therefore, nutrition study becomes an important aspect that brooks no negligence in discussions on socioeconomic development strategies and policies. As far as China's poverty alleviation program is concerned, the first step should be directed at solving the problem of food shortages for the poor. Studies on the nutrition status of the poor will help us understand whether the problem has been resolved. As compared with the indicator of per capita grain ration in use now, nutrition indicators can reflect the extent of food security more accurately.

Based on the above understanding, the authors conducted diet survey by making use of questionnaires answered by housewives. Owing to the fact that the poor do not take in many kinds of food and farmers' families in the same area have almost homogeneous food composition, the design of the diet survey becomes very simple: housewives are enquired about number of people eating at home, varieties of food consumption, and amount of consumption three days before the interview. It is not as strict as the nutrition surveys done by the Nutrition Research Institute of the Chinese Academy of Preventative Medical Sciences. Yet it can roughly display disparities of sample households in nutrition status and discrepancies of households in different areas under research in food security.

Methods provided by the Nutrition Research Institute are utilized to process the data. First, the average amount of nutrient intake of sample households per reference person per day is figured out. Reference person is converted in accordance with sex, age, and physical activities of each family member (for the conversion rates, see Table 1 in Appendix) so as to remove the influence of these factors on the amount of diet intake of an individual and make sure that people with differing features share one common comparable base. For example, a 15-year-old boy is tantamount to the unit of one reference person, while a 16-year-old girl equals one reference person; the conversion rate of a boy at 10 is 0.875, while that of a girl at the same age is 0.833; for laborers with high physical intensity aged between 17 and 45 years old, man is converted into 1.417 reference person and woman 1.250. The data from the survey also include information on guests. Number of people eating at home and amount of food intake minus the number of guests and their amount of food consumption, respectively, enables us to calculate for each family the average amount of diet intake per reference person per day. Then, in line with nutritional ingredients of each kind of food consumed, we can figure out the amount of nutrients intake of an average reference person per day.

Here, the amount of nutrients provision in everyday diet recommended in October 1988 by the China Nutrition Society is referred to as the basis for the assessment of nutritional status of sample households (Institute of Nutrition of the Chinese Academy of Preventive Medical Science 1991). The amount of nutrients provision is different from that of requirement. The latter indicates the amount needed to maintain normal physiologic functions of human body. While the former includes considerations of individual differences in order to guarantee that overwhelming majority of people can get the amount of nutrients required. If the average nutrients intake of a certain group of people is lower than the amount of provision recommended, then we conclude that some individuals in the group have inadequate intake of nutrients. The larger the two figures differ, the higher the ratio of undernourished people it means. The Nutrition Society recommends that a reference person should absorb 2,400 kilocalories of energy per day, of which fat energy reaches 20-25 percent; protein intake should top 70-80 grams, 11-14 percent of total energy, and carbohydrates at 60-70 percent.

Table 7.2 shows the nutritional status of sample households divided into groups in accordance with per capita disposable income. It does not include all nutrients taken in by the population under study. Instead it only lists the most common indices: energy, fat, and protein intakes. The percentage of energy provided by fat and protein demonstrates the quality of diet. The data in the Table reveals:

1. Under most circumstances, in the same area, households with higher income enjoy better nutritional status.

2. There exist remarkable regional differences in the nutritional status of rural households. Of the three counties, only nutrient quantity and quality absorbed by families in Linqu county basically meet the recommended provision criteria. Though energy intake in Wangcang county is the largest, the shares of energy provided by fat and protein for the middle- and low-income groups are lower than recommended standards. The households in Xiji county experience the worst nutrition status. Their nutrient intake is lower than that in the other two counties even though they are on the same income level. Judging by the recommended nutrition standards, most families are undernourished.

Table 7.2—Average nutrition intake per reference person per day of sample households

Income Group[a]	Number of Households	Energy Intake	Energy[b] from Fat	from Protein	Intake of Protein
		(kilocalories)	(percent)	(percent)	(grams)
Linqu/Shandong	120	2,389	21.9	13.8	82
First group	2	2,208	19.8	12.8	71
Second group	42	2,430	20.3	13.1	80
Third group	38	2,335	22.1	13.7	80
Fourth group	20	2,562	22.1	13.7	88
Fifth group	18	2,238	24.8	16.0	89
Xiji/Ningxia	120	1,547	14.7	11.4	44
First group	29	1,457	13.8	11.0	40
Second group	51	1,536	14.0	11.3	43
Third group	22	1,730	15.6	12.2	53
Fourth group	11	1,431	14.8	11.4	41
Fifth group	7	1,604	19.4	11.6	46
Wangcang/Sichuan	118	3,368	21.2	10.0	84
First group	7	3,355	14.4	9.2	77
Second group	21	3,364	14.9	8.9	75
Third group	24	3,385	15.9	9.3	78
Fourth group	14	3,579	18.3	9.8	87
Fifth group	52	3,306	28.1	11.0	91

[a] Groups are divided in accordance with household per capita disposable income: the first group, <200 yuan; second group, 201-400 yuan; third group, 401-600 yuan; fourth group, 601-800 yuan; and the fifth group, > 800 yuan.

[b] The conversion rates of energy in food are calculated in accordance with the following formula, namely

protein:fat:carbohydrate (per gram) = 4:9:4 (kilocalories).

See Tables of Food Ingredients compiled by the Institute of Nutrition of the Chinese Academy of Preventive Medical Science (1991), People's Health Care Publishing House, Beijing.

Table 7.3—Quality and energy composition of diet of sample households[a]

Sources of Energy (Types of Food)	Linqu/Shandong			Xiji/Ningxia			Wangcang/Sichuan		
	Type 1	Type 2	Type 3	Type 1	Type 2	Type 3	Type 1	Type 2	Type 3
	(percent)								
Cereal and rhizome	81.3	86.7	81.5	89.7	83.7	89.2	74.2	80.0	86.0
Meat	2.9	2.3	2.4	3.0	4.0	0.7	6.3	6.4	5.2
Additional fat	5.0	4.1	7.4	3.9	4.2	5.9	6.5	3.6	0.8
Beans and bean products	0.4	0.2	0.8	0.1	2.7	2.4	1.1	0.3	1.3
Sugar	0.3	0.4	0.4	0.2	0.1	0.2	0.6	0.6	0.1
Nut oil	0.0	0.0	0.0	0.0	0.0	0.0	0.0	0.0	0.0
Vegetables and fruits	10.1	6.3	7.5	3.1	5.3	1.6	11.3	9.1	6.6
Wine and soft drinks	0.0	0.0	0.0	0.0	0.0	0.0	0.0	0.0	0.0
Total	100.0	100.0	100.0	100.0	100.0	100.0	100.0	100.0	100.0
Desirable dietary pattern (DDP) points[b]	73.6	63.1	70.6	57.9	71.6	56.9	85.1	78.9	70.2

[a] Sample households are divided into groups in line with types of villages.

[b] Diet quality points are also referred to as points of desirable dietary pattern, the calculation method of which can be found in Food Consumption and Nutritional Status of Farmers in Six Provinces and One Municipality included in the research reports of Chinese Academy of Preventive Medical Sciences prepared by Chen Chunming and others.

All nutrition indices in Table 7.2 have been calculated on the basis of the same data, that is, on three-day recalls of rural women on household food consumption. The survey was carried out in the middle of the farming season in Linqu and Wangcang Counties, when the diet of farmers was of better quality than average. In Xiji County, the survey was carried out during the off-season, when the level of food consumption was comparatively low. These seasonal conditions led to an overestimation of the indices for Linqu and Wangcang Counties and an underestimation of indices for Xiji County. Besides, the disparity in rural women's estimations of weights of consumed food in different areas might also have led to further errors.

However, it is necessary to note the observation on food consumption of the sample households in order to achieve a better understanding about the nutrition status of the rural poor in China:

1. The staple foods constitute the main part of the diet of the sample households. Staple for inhabitants in Linqu County is wheat flour, and that in Wangcang County, rice. Maize and potatoes are the staple foods for farmers in Xiji County. Energy, fat, and protein contained in the first two kinds of food are higher than those in the latter two.

2. There are marked differences in the extent of diet diversification for the households among the three studied counties (see Table 7.3). Households in Linqu and Wangcang Counties absorb more nutrients from vegetables and fruits than people in Xiji County. Not only do the former consume more greenstuff than the latter, they also eat fresh vegetables in season. While the latter often eat pickled radish and cabbage together with staple food.

3. The above-mentioned differences in diet quantity and quality for the households in different areas are determined by climate, irrigation, ecological environment, and market conditions. Wangcang County, located in South China, enjoys a temperate climate with abundant rainfall that is conducive to growing rice, vegetables, and other cereals. Compared with the counties of Linqu and Xiji, situated in North China, grain production per mu in Wangcang County is up 33 percent and 55 percent, respectively (see Table 3.2). Because of plentiful fodder, every household raises pigs. As a result, traditional homemade bacon becomes the major animal food.

Though climate in Linqu County is not as favorable as that in Wangcang County, well-developed irrigation system there partly offsets such defect. Transport facilities, in particular, make local trade there more prosperous than in Wangcang County. Farmers always barter dried sweet potatoes with peddlers for rice and vegetables so as to improve diet consumption of families.

By contrast, social and economic conditions related to food provision in Xiji County are not at all favorable: though per capita arable land of a household averagely accounted for three times as many as that in the other two counties, the land productivity is the lowest, which is an outcome of long-standing deterioration of the ecological environment. In order to satisfy the normal nutrients requirement of an individual under existing circumstances, much more arable land than that needed by the other two counties has to be employed. This implies that as far as energy intake is concerned, a household in Xiji County has to pay higher prices than that in the other two counties in order to acquire every kilocalorie of energy.

Wheat in Xiji County often cannot survive due to lack of water. As a result, potatoes, which are most drought-resistant, become one of the staple foods in farmers' families. Most of beans and peas are for sale and become a major source of cash income for families. Though households with higher income enjoy better nutritional status than low-income groups in the county, they have to take account of expenses on nonfood necessities, such as fuel, clothing, and medicine, etc. So they still suffer from undernourishment as compared with households on the same level of income in other areas. This shows exactly that income is by no means the only determinant of nutrition.

Since 1988, farmers participating in the Yigong-daizhen projects were paid in "industrial product coupons," redeemable only for commodities purchased in appointed state-owned shops. Earnings from projects, although they reinforced the purchasing power of participating rural households, have not necessarily played a decisive role in determining the nutritional status of rural families. This is because farm households do not rely on purchases for food consumption, for the most part. Moreover, the projects' earnings were

Table 7.4—Nutritional situation of participating and nonparticipating households[a] (sample households), China

	Linqu/Shandong		Xiji/Ningxia		Wangcang/Sichuan	
	Participating Households N=58	Non-Participating Households N=62	Participating Households N=39	Non-Participating Households N=81	Participating Households N=64	Non-Participating Households N=54
Calorie intake[b] per person	2,423	2,358	1,708	1,469 (2,600)	3,490 (2,212)	3,223
Supplied by fat (percent)	22.2	21.7	14.9 (13.3)	14.6 (15.3)	22.1	20.1
Supplied by protein (percent)	14.3	13.3	11.7 (10.8)	11.3 (11.5)	10.3	9.6
Protein intake (grams)	86.7	78.3	49.9 (70.5)	41.4 (63.4)	90.1	77.1
Diet quality points[c]	87.8	84.8	67.0	66.8	82.5	77.2

[a] Method of calculation: see The Institute of Nutrition of the Chinese Academy of Preventive Medical Science, *The Table of Food Components*, published by the People's Health Publishing House.

[b] Data in parentheses have been calculated according to sample household per capita amount of yearly food consumption, while the others are from three-day recalls on food consumption amounts in the survey season.

[c] The "diet quality points" can also be termed as "points of desired diet pattern." Regarding methods of calculation, see Chen Chunming (1992).

mainly spent on nonfood consumer goods (Chapter 6.3). So, although Table 7.4 indicates that the nutritional status of households participating in the projects is better than that of those not participating, this difference may not be due to their different participation decisions. To explore the factors affecting the nutritional situation of rural families, the quality of diet of every sample household was assessed, using the formula of Desired Diet Pattern Points designed by the Chinese Academy of Preventative Medical Science (see appendix).

All indices in Table 7.4, except calorie and protein intake, closely conform to the results of surveys made by the Chinese Academy of Preventative Medical Sciences (Chen Chumming 1992). As far as the points of rural household diet quality are concerned, the Academy has given Ningxia 69.8 points and Sichuan 75.5 points (Shandong Province was not covered in the survey). So, it was decided to use the existing data on the nutritional situation of sample households as the basis for the analysis in this chapter.

Compared with calorie, fat, and protein intake, diet quality points are a more comprehensive index of nutritional situation. This method of scoring points overcomes the problem of simplification that occurs when nutritional situation is estimated on the basis of single components. Because they have this advantage, diet quality points are used as dependent variables in the regression analysis.

Through regression analyses, explanatory variables were identified. These are the household per capita predicted income (PREDINC), the predicted income squared (PREDINC2), and—representing, to some extent, dietary diversity—the number of poultry kept by the household (POULTRY):

$$NUTRIT = 62.817 + 0.16E\text{-}01\ PREDINC - 0.31E\text{-}05\ PREDINC2 +$$
$$\quad\quad\quad (20.731)\quad\quad\quad (3.890)^{**}\quad\quad\quad\quad (-1.987)^{**}$$

$$0.30\ EDUCW + 0.44\ POULTRY - 0.36\ FNUMHH$$
$$(1.112)\quad\quad\quad (4.545)^{**}\quad\quad\quad (-0.740)$$

$$R^2 = 0.174\quad F\,(5,\,352) = 14.884\quad N = 358.$$

Factors affecting the nutritional situation of the population are quite complicated. The regression analysis here has only identified some of the significant variables—higher per capita income, and comparatively, abundant farming products. In addition, predicted income squared appeared to be negatively linked to a family's nutritional status, implying that the diet quality scores would not go further up when income reaches a certain level. The number of years spent in school by women (EDUCW) and household size (FNUMHH) did not seem to be significant factors in determining nutritional levels in the sample. The positive relation of the former variable (women's level of education) with diet quality is consistent with the observations of the authors in the case studies. Due to the division of labor among family members, the education level of rural women relates closely to the success of the livestock business, and is of key importance in the rationalization of the family food consumption and nutrient intakes.

POLICY IMPLICATIONS OF RESEARCH RESULTS

The research reported in this chapter provides some insights relevant to policymaking:

•   Food consumption constitutes the biggest component of expenditure in sample households, and is determined mainly by family farming products. This relationship is as expected in the low-income economy of the sample households.
•   General malnutrition persists in the poor counties (such as Xiji County) of the less-developed provinces, indicating that food security has not yet been achieved for the inhabitants in these areas. The nutritional intake of the population in poor counties of more developed provinces (Linqu and Wangcang Counties) has reached the average level of the nation (Chen Chumming 1992). The problem of food shortages in these areas has been solved.
•   Farmers' earnings from Yigong-daizhen projects may not play a direct role in the improvement of food consumption and nutritional situation of rural families, but the project itself has indirect impacts on them. The regression analysis of nutritional situation shows that rural household per

capita income is as important determinant. Project earnings influence the nutritional situation through a chain of indirect effects:

a. Rural household per capita income is much determined by village infrastructure conditions. The improvement of infrastructure was a major objective of the Yigong-daizhen projects prior to 1991.

b. Starting in 1991, investments for the projects have concentrated on farmland and water conservancy capital construction to increase crop yields and, hence, strengthen food security through improved food availability and income.

Village committees and local governments are more qualified to set project priorities based on whether villages are better served with infrastructure or land and water resource-focused projects or a mix of the two.

8

DISCUSSION OF RESEARCH RESULTS

This chapter contains a concentrated discussion on the results of the analyses in Chapters 5-7. First of all, the characteristics of the Yigong-daizhen projects will be reviewed through international comparisons, to be followed by an exploration on the limits of project effects in terms of poverty alleviation as well as on problems existing in their organizational and operational patterns. Finally, measurements for improvement are to be suggested.

EFFECTS OF YIGONG-DAIZHEN PROJECTS

Economic growth has been the hot issue to which Chinese economists paid great concern during the past 10 years and more, while the social development has been habitually neglected in their discussions. The tendency may originate in the thinking that without economic growth, there would be no strength to support social development. The idea is not that wrong, but is one-sided, because social development should be the purpose of economic growth. If this point should be neglected in decisionmaking, there would be the danger of being misled towards the drawback of "growth without development." Historical experiences at home and abroad have proved that economic growth does not necessarily mean social development. And the poverty alleviation and better livelihood of the entire population still needs the efforts of government interventions through income redistribution and public investment. According to the experience of a number of developing countries since World War II, internationally noted scholars divided social development strategies into two categories, "growth-mediated" and "support-led" (Drèze and Sen 1989). Although there was high-speed economic growth in Brazil during the 1960s, due to its extremely unequal income distribution and high rate of poverty incidence, it was regarded as typical of the states having neglected social development. Meanwhile, South Korea was taken as the representative of a state adopting "growth-mediated" strategy in social development, because its social policy was carried out after having achieved a certain extent of abundance. China and Sri Lanka were deemed as examples of states taking the "support-led" strategy in their social development, because both of them had resorted to government intervention to improve their social services and to markedly raise the living standard of their populations, even before their respective entrance into the ranks of effective medium-income countries. The antipoverty measures of the Chinese Government starting from the mid-1980s can be seen as a continuation of the tradition of public support.

Unlike the practice in the past when sheer relief was extended to the poor, the policy of poverty alleviation during the reform lay emphasis on assisting the poor to bring into play their own potential, which coincides exactly the characteristics of Yigong-daizhen project designs. First of all, the projects and techniques used are so selected as to be appropriate to the conditions of resources in poor regions. The road and drinking water installation construction as stated above are examples of such projects capable of utilizing not only local materials but also the local labor force. The simple and labor-intensive technique used were within the reach of the local laborers so that a large amount of surplus labor was able to get to work during the implementation of the projects.

Second, the system of multiple participation in the implementation of the projects has motivated the initiatives of both local governments and the masses of people in poor regions. Taking the project investments as an example, the system has been able to pool together the disposable resources of both the central and local governments and of the village communities and farmers, thus giving play to economy of scale through concentrated utilization of all factors (capitals, land, labor, and so forth). The lower rate of capital returns in poor regions vis-à-vis the national average had generally weakened its competitiveness in attracting investment, even more so in the case of infrastructural constructions. Under such considerations, the investment from the Central Government have played the role of "first drive," pushing the local governments to pool together as possible the local resources and actively organize the implementation of the projects. That is to say, factors put in from outside by the Central Government have set in motion the existing capacity in poor regions. Without the inducement and initiation of an amount of this primary capital, the scattered local capital would not be possibly amassed in such a high speed while the rich natural construction materials and abundant labor can only remain the resources lying fast asleep.

Summing up the results of analyses in the preceding chapters, it can be confirmed that the Yigong-daizhen projects characteristic of their labor-intensive techniques have brought into play the advantages of abundant labor resource of poor regions, helped the improvement of regional infrastructure and social services, and increased the job opportunities and incomes for the poor. However, due to the differences between ordinary poor and extremely poor regions, the impacts of the projects also differ in different particular aspects. In areas where the problem of food shortage has no more been a serious threat, the Yigong-daizhen projects in infrastructural constructions have activated local economic growth. During the implementation of the projects, about one-half of the labor inputs were obligatory workdays of farmers. This kind of practice presupposes two conditions: first, the recognition of the farmers' obligation to participate in public investments through labor accumulation and, second, an existing income of the farmers, capable of meeting their basic requirements of subsistence. It is in the extremely poor regions that farmers' income from the projects are imbued essentially with the meaning of relief. It is because that even without the projects, the state civil administrative departments would continue to provide relief to poor households in such regions. Any improvement in social services in project areas undoubtedly signifies a kind of development.

So, it can be said that the policy of Yigong-daizhen has organically combined the three components of relief, economic growth, and social development together.

However, this research also proves that the effect of the policy of Yigong-daizhen does have its limits, which lies in the following aspects:

• The projects cannot simultaneously cover all of the poor regions because of the limitation of disposable resources. Besides the craftsmen, laborers in the nonproject villages find it difficult to obtain the opportunities of joining the projects and obtaining wages, though being poor.

• The jobs and earnings directly brought to farmers through the projects are of a short-term nature. Once the projects are completed, this source of income for farmers of the project villages will soon be lost.

• Although the improvement of infrastructure is helpful to increase household income in project areas, not all the households there can really achieve income increase. Even in the same village and under similar infrastructural conditions, there can be differences among the nonpoor, poor, and extremely poor households, apparently, due to personal reasons. For the poor, a long-term and gainful employment constitutes a prerequisite for a stable income sufficient to maintain their subsistence, which, in turn, depends upon the poverty alleviation projects in the fields of direct productions as well as on the investments in human resources.

Then it is obvious that the public works has created only one of many essential conditions for alleviation and elimination of poverty, while the poor need help in all aspects of culture, education, health care, and production. Only by taking long-term and comprehensive investment can the poverty be gradually and stably alleviated. Perhaps this is true to most developing countries.

The distinct feature of public works in China lies in its targeting mechanisms. In the process of carrying out Yigong-daizhen projects, the Chinese Government did not use the "self-targeting" mechanisms. Instead, it selected the beneficiaries of the projects through adjusting project sites and investment orientations. Now that the targeting mechanisms of the Yigong-daizhen projects are determined by both the institutional arrangement of the existing socioeconomic system of rural society and the target designs of policy, some characteristics different from the targeting mechanisms of public works in other developing countries arise therefrom. These are:

1. The Yigong-daizhen program in China has been designed primarily for alleviation of regional poverty, hence, characterized with regional targeting mechanisms. Therefore, it does not necessarily target the poorest. The primary purpose of carrying out the projects is to improve the infrastructure and social service of poor regions and to create conditions for regional economic growth. In other words, compared with the increase of short-term job opportunities and supplementary incomes for the poor, the long-term targets of economic growth are in a position of precedence. It is exactly because of this that the principle of efficiency has been carried out throughout the process of decisionmaking and construction of projects with the rate of success being carefully run after. The practice certainly cannot ensure the extremely poor villages and the poorest to be the first to benefit because the villages in extreme poverty used to be in the areas with less investment advantages.

2. Within the framework of poor regions, it is the village communities, but not the individual households or persons, that are targeted by the projects. During the implementation of the projects, the village communities are responsible for mobilization of the labor force. And after the completion, the projects would assume the shape of either the village communities' public infrastructure (roads, for example) or the properties of the village communities (such as the water supply installations), or the added values of existing properties of village communities (such as terraced fields constructed and soils improved), and others. Thus, it is obviously impossible to exclude the nonpoor from being beneficiaries of the projects.

This distinguishing feature of the targeting mechanisms of Yigong-daizhen projects has been determined by the organizational pattern of the current rural society in China as well as its institutional arrangements. During the transitional period from the centrally planned economy to a market economy, the village community becomes a self-governing body in the rural society while its administrative organ, the villager committee, plays the role as a bridge connecting the government and peasant households, in addition to its duty of responsibility for the public affairs in the village. As a kind of government investment behavior absorbing a large amount of peasant households in the course of its implementation, the Yigong-daizhen projects would be difficult to run smoothly without the media of village communities. Furthermore, due to the principle of equity practiced in village communities and the fact that most of the households in the villages of poor regions belong to the poor, the village communities are more helpful than any other kind of agents to enable the projects benefiting the poor. If individual brokers were trusted to recruit the labor force, those who benefit mostly would possibly be the brokers themselves and the nonpoor. This is because the laborers with highest mobility are presently not the poor, whose activities are usually limited within the scope of their own local villages or townships due to their disability in paying the traveling expenses.

Besides, the contents of the projects also facilitate the village communities to be a beneficial unit. As early as the time of the Communes, the grassroots social services were first established at the level of production brigades. During the rural economic reforms, the social functions of the production brigades have transferred to the village communities. What is more important is that the land has now been owned by the village communities, thus effectively strengthening their connections with peasant households. It is clear that the project-controlling departments concerned have taken village communities as the fundamental beneficial units of the projects, no matter whether the project is designed for investing in farmland capital construction or improving grassroots social services.

This does not necessarily mean that the poverty alleviation projects in China all target village communities. Now that the peasant households have been transformed into basic production units, the targets of credit projects with subsidized interest lent for extension of advanced techniques in cropping production and for development of animal husbandry and processing sectors, are usually individual households.

3. The operational pattern of the projects combining regional targeting and a labor force mobilization with village community involvement has taken account of both "efficiency" and "equity," thus enabling the poor to be finally the majority of the beneficiaries.

CURRENT PROBLEMS IN IMPLEMENTATING PROJECTS AND TENTATIVE SOLUTIONS

Based on the analysis of the targeting mechanisms of the Yigong-daizhen projects, it can be inferred that a considerable amount of extremely poor villages were excluded from the beneficiaries during the implementation of road and drinking water installation projects. Although among all the poor villages there must be an order of priorities in getting benefits, it should not be allowed to freely continue such a state of affairs, still less to let it become a fixed pattern. Therefore, it is necessary to extend the coverage of the projects towards the extremely poor villages, even early at the time of making investment plans. The farmland capital construction scheme starting from 1991 has set its major projects in the stone mountain areas, deep mountain areas, and high and cold mountain areas. It can be predicted that such Yigong-daizhen projects will be able to target the poorest crowd. Furthermore, even when public works such as road building are not carried out in extremely poor villages, the directing groups of the projects should take measures to consciously create opportunities for laborers in such villages to take part in the projects. Examples for this may include the stipulation of a certain share of overall participants of the projects to be the laborers from extremely poor villages. This facilitates the circulation of the labor force, the gradual abolition of barriers among and between village communities, and the improvement of the quality of manpower resources in the extremely poor villages through the participation.

The selection of beneficiaries through the adjustment of project sites and investment orientations represents the traditional way of resource allocation by the system of central planning. Presently, the Chinese economy in the transitional period exists both as sections regulated by the market and sections controlled by the plan. The Yigong-daizhen projects belong to the latter, with its operation still bearing the characteristic of a commanding economy being controlled through documents transmitted down to the grassroots level from the central leadership, along the hierarchy of administrative ranks. The allocation of resource among different areas and different programs, the allotment and transportation of commodities, the financial administration and supervision, and so on, are all strictly stipulated in the documents. Though the practice has the advantage of preventing the investments from having leakages, yet it does have shortcomings of rigidity in making plans from above and of being at times beyond the requirements of the local populace. Village communities diverting funds for farmland capital construction to build roads, discovered by the authors during the research, represents one example. It is conceivable that during the period when roads and drinking water installations were planned as the major projects, village communities with serious food shortages might give the terraced field construction first priority if they were competent to make such a choice.

Such being the case, if the "top-to-bottom" procedure of decisionmaking were converted to one of "bottom-to-top," would not the problem thus be solved? But things are not so simple like that. The way of "bottom-to-top" presupposes the democratization of decisionmaking without which and without a system of market reference; it might turn out to be, for the central planning system, a kind of decisionmaking process with higher transaction costs. Schemes of resource allocation for Yigong-daizhen projects have usually been the outcome of compromises reached at the arbitration of higher-level governments following interregional and intersectoral scrambles for great quotas of investments. Presently, the feasible measure for rectification of the existing procedure is the further decentralization of decisionmaking. It is for the Central Government to stipulate the floating margin of the proportion among different projects in the division of investments, thus giving local governments and village communities more room for making choices.

Knowing the defects of the planned economy, why, then, the authors suggest to control investment orientation through administrative means? The reason is that the Yigong-daizhen projects have been, so far, carried out through government institutions and, owing to the lack of public supervision and others systems of checks and balances, the conduct of government officials can only be regulated by administrative instructions. The public infrastructural constructions are nonprofit undertakings. Without any regulation for the use of investments, the goods and materials allotted for the purpose may possibly be diverted to other sectors with higher capital returns.

One of the important contents of the Chinese economic reform is the change of government functions, that is, the government must withdraw from the activities of the enterprises and limit its functions, particularly in dealing with public social affairs and macroeconomic managements. Such a goal has not yet been fully realized. Officials of the economic functional departments and leading members of local governments have still played, to different extents, the role of entrepreneurs and their achievements being gauged by the results of economic activities of their respective localities or departments. In the situation of a serious shortage of public investments in poor regions, the functional departments of local governments have been pressing hard to get Yigong-daizhen projects so as to win an additional part of the resources. Their requirements from different areas and departments met together to form a pressure transmitted to the Central Government, which was further reinforced by the huge social effects of the road and drinking water installation projects during the 1980s. It was under this background that the Central Government made the decision to fix the Yigong-daizhen as a medium, long-term policy for poverty alleviation. Since the first years of the 1990s, not only have the commodities allotted for the Yigong-daizhen projects increased, but the area of implementation also has expanded. Up to the year 1993, four Yigong-daizhen schemes have been assigned by the State Planning Commission. These are:

• 1,500 million yuan' worth of industrial products to be used in the drinking water installation projects, road building projects, and farmland capital construction projects during 1990-92;

• 5,000 million yuan' worth of foodgrains to be used in farmland capital construction projects during the period 1991-95;

• 10,000 million yuan' worth of industrial products and foodgrains to be used in harnessing projects of big rivers during the period 1991-95;

•   10,000 million yuan' worth of foodgrains, cloth, edible oil. and other me-
dium- and low-grade industrial products to be used in the rural infrastructural construction during the period 1993-97.

It is expected that the expansion of investments will speed up the improvement of infrastructure in the middle and western poor regions. But due
to the cross implementation of many Yigong-daizhen projects during a same
period and the marked increase in the number of invested sectors, a series of
new problems have arisen, which include reduction in economy of scale in
terms of resource use, increasingly complicated organizational systems of
the projects, and the weakening of effects of the investment for poverty alleviation.

1. The projects of harnessing big rivers are essentially the investments in
kind in large-scale water conservancy construction made by the Central
Government following the 1991 flood. The projects are characteristic of
their high technical standard with strict time limits and are constructed
mainly by professional construction companies, while most of the benefited
areas are nonpoor regions. The workers and staffs for the projects are
mostly from the cities and are paid in cash as usual. Input goods used by the
projects are supplied through purchases. This is because the materials allotted by the government are not the needs of the projects. Thus, huge gaps
in investments arise that local governments are unwilling to fill and also un-
able to fill in time with enough funds. All of these show that the style of operation of Yigong-daizhen projects does not suit such programs. Yet, the
program still bears the name of "Yigong-daizhen" projects despite its lack of
poverty alleviation characteristics, which gives rise to the discontent of local
governments of poor regions and intensifies the contradictions among different regions in the scramble of investments.

2. Yigong-daizhen projects have now extended to the fields of agriculture, forestry, water conservancy, transportation, communication, commerce, education, health, and others. Now the contents of projects cover not
only road building, farmland and water conservancy capital construction,
but also new tasks of afforestation and renovation of rural post offices, purchase and supply cooperatives, health and sanitation centers, old school-

houses in danger, and so on. As a result, the project executive institutions have also extended to involve more than 10 government functional departments, thus making the coordination among these departments more and more difficult. Everyone of them contends hard for more projects and all of them are in a difficult condition to fulfill their plans due to insufficient resources, thus resulting in an awkward situation of increases in the number of half-done projects.

3. Increase in the number of projects causes the rapid expansion of requirements for matching funds of the local, which, in turn, further intensifies the shortage of local financial resources. To fill the gap in investments, more and more goods and materials allotted from the Central Government, originally to be used for payments to farmers working for the projects, have been transferred either into currencies or directly into invested goods by the local governments of the project areas. Such a state of affairs has occurred continuously in spite of repeated prohibitions by the Central Government, resulting in the lowering of wages for farmers, weakening the project's color of poverty alleviation, and making the role of the projects daily approaching simply a kind of capital construction investment.

For the same reason, the county and township governments have resorted to the increase of obligatory workdays (a labor taxation in essence) to narrow the gap in investments, which may possibly make the poor even poorer due to the reduction of gainful employment opportunities during the period of implementation of the projects.

4. In certain areas, there exists the problem of serious damages in public installations (especially roads), due to a lack of maintenance systems after the completion of the projects, which has resulted in the reappearance of difficulties in transportation, drinking water supplies, and so on. The reason for this, according to local officials, lies mainly in the lack of funds necessary for maintenance of established projects.

The problems listed above come mainly from the existing defects of the planned economy, while also having relations with the impact of the present-day market economy, the normal order of which remains yet to be established. So, the problems are now impossible to be fundamentally solved within the framework of regulation of the planned economy. It is the reforms in the socioeconomic structures and in the decisionmaking procedures that are decisive to have the defects uprooted. However, during the process of reform, only the coordinated use of both the long-term and short-term measures can be resorted to for the correction of planning failures whenever they happen.

The practice of making capital construction investments in kind in nonpoor regions under the name of "Yigong-daizhen" can be regarded as nothing but unreasonable decisionmaking in the disposal of resources resulted from the prevailing practices of "Zhangguan-yizhi" (decisionmaking solely according to the will of the senior officials) under conditions of serious imperfect information.

The "Yigong-daizhen" before the 1980s had been a way of government relief for those affected by natural calamities. Of course, a disaster area does not necessarily mean a poor area. The particular sense of poverty alleviation was imbued into the Yigong-daizhen program since the year 1985, when the antipoverty strategy of the Chinese Government started its operation. So, the traditional way of relief through public works after big disasters should not be negated even now as an effective measure. The problem is that such an emergency assistance in nonpoor regions has been played up as investment schemes in kind with a term as long as five years so that not only its meaning of relief and poverty alleviation has thus been lost, the practice itself also runs contrary to the tendency of market-oriented reforms. During the transition period towards market economy, both the units carrying out the investments and the wage workers should have more sovereignty in selection of commodities with money so as to enable optimum resource allocation to be realized through price signals.

Furthermore, there always have been surplus products here and there under the planned economy because "plans" can never catch up with the "changes" of the real economy. However, with the ever-growing sovereignty of consumers during the course of marketization, products failing to meet the demand in market, but still in the field of supply, regulated by the planned economy, have increased relatively, thus intensifying the situation of surpluses in one or several kinds of products in certain periods of time. To enable the producers, especially the state-owned enterprises, to produce in line with demand in market, it needs further institutional reforms. In this background, the practice since 1985 of using surplus foodgrains and daily consumer goods for Yigong-daizhen projects in poor regions has shown its effects in easing of the pressure of heavy stockpiles of the state, in partially meeting the basic needs of the poor and in the infrastructural construction, thus achieving huge social benefits unexpected to the planners. However, the information, as such, transmitted upward to high-level decisionmakers were so distorted that various premises to the success were neglected, such as the low wage rates in poor regions, the reasons causing the poor to accept payments in kind and others, which might have misled decisionmakers into thinking that the Yigong-daizhen program is the best choice for the disposal of overstocks of the state and a type of investment with lower cost, suitable for all public work constructions. Hence, the decision for making investments in the big river and big lake flood preventative projects under the name and with the operation type of the Yigong-daizhen program were made.

If there were effective check and balance systems, errors described above might be reduced. But, for present decisionmakers, it is only the supervision from higher ranks that are useful, while restrictions on the top-level decisionmakers are very limited indeed. Even when mistakes in decisionmaking are discovered, the people at the lower rank will, in most cases, preferably avoid making any critics so as to maintain their existing positions and also for the sake of future promotions. So, the feasible way today to straighten up decisionmaking errors may lie in the improvement of the feedback system of information through nongovernmental evaluation on the investments. To supervise Yigong-daizhen investments through the People's Congress may not be that difficult at township and county levels, but the transaction costs will be too high in making supervision against decisionmaking at central and provincial levels. It is because in comparison with overall public investments at these two levels, the resources put in the Yigong-daizhen projects are almost negligible.

The situation of the continuous increase of sectors in poor regions taking part in the distribution of Yigong-daizhen resources, the rapid expansion of gaps in investments, the downward efficiency in the utilization of resources,

and so on, are all inevitable problems of the planned economy, while both
the success and defects shown in the course of implementation of Yigong-
daizhen policies reflect a miniature of the Chinese macroeconomy in the
transitional state. That is to say, the way of operation of the projects, while
maintaining the characteristics of the planned economy, varies due to the
reforms in traditional decisionmaking procedures and the introduction of the
market mechanisms.

1. Under the traditional planning system, the practice of investment
without risks has encouraged officials in the executive departments to increase, by all possible means, new projects, thus causing the gap between
investment requirements and real funds available to be the headache of the
economy. Further, the decentralization in making decisions also has intensified the contradictions between the central and local governments on the
issue of allocation of resources. In the development of the system of multiple
participation in investments, both sides intentionally leave gaps in their respective investment portions, which grow in scale from the higher level
downward, to be filled finally in a port by the obligatory workdays of farmers, on the one hand, and the newly added investments, on the other, obtained through the requests of grassroots governments with half-done projects being their weights in their bargaining with higher authorities.

2. Under the background of the coexistence of diversified price systems
at present and of the fact that investment plans assigned by the Central
Government are made according to government fixed prices, the fluctuations
in real prices during the course of implementation have made the executive
organs difficult to get sufficient goods and materials necessary for the projects or to be profited through rent-seeking activities.

(3) The goods and materials allotted according to regular infrastructural investment plans should be those needed by the projects, such as steel products, cement, and other capital goods, but not foodgrains or other consumer
goods. So, when there exists the situation as the points (1) and (2) stated
above, the monetization of the originally invested goods in the Yigong-
daizhen projects become unavoidable.

Measures for rectification lie at the starting point of the problem. According to the survey made by the authors, when executive units were lim-

ited in only a few functional departments (for example, the two departments of transportation and water conservancy), the situation as state above was not that serious and was easy to be controlled due to the simplicity of the operations. It is obvious that if the area of Yigong-daizhen investments during a same plan period were narrowed down and the number of executive departments cut, there would be a renewal of the efficiencies. But in such cases, all functional departments concerned would put forward ample arguments to convince their leading institutions not to elbow them out of the fields, with everyone of them emphasizing the area under his (or her) leadership as that of first importance to have the investments.

If the planning department at the higher level is to make the final decision, it might be, once again, a repetition of the defect of inflexibility of the planned economy as described at the beginning of this chapter. To get out of this vicious circle, it can only depend on the introduction of elements of democratic decisionmaking. While making investment plans, it would be the duty of the central planning department to define the fields of investments for choice and to stipulate that investments can be made only in one or two sectors during a same plan period, which is to be decided through the voting of the People's Congress at the county level. This is because investment plans will be finally implemented by county-level functional departments.

The behavior of the project executive departments in converting the goods and materials allotted by the Central Government into currencies or capital goods shows that it is necessary to merge the infrastructural construction by Yigong-daizhen projects in poor regions into regular public investment programs of the Central Government. The practice of disposing surplus products through Yigong-daizhen projects will become gradually unsuitable for poor regions. Among the households participating in the projects involved in this research, those who prefer a payment in cash make up more than four-fifths of the total. This result of the sample statistics also proves the above inference.

The maintenance expenses of the established projects should depend directly or indirectly upon the receipts from users of the completed works. The practice of drinking water supply installations in Sichuan Province represents an example of this. But governments and farmers of a considerable part of the poor counties still habitually depend on appropriations of higher-level governments without any idea of receiving payments for the use of public installations and resources (water, for example). Besides, even with sufficient appropriations, the maintenance of public works also depends on strict regulations and the abidance of the users to the disciplines.

After all, the defects arising from the planned economy can only be uprooted through reform of the system itself while, during the transition period, some expedient measures for the improvement of decisionmaking procedures are also necessary so as to correct planning failures.

9

MACRO-ECONOMIC CONSTRAINTS
ON ANTI-POVERTY PROGRAMS

During the past 10 years and more, the Chinese economy was operating essentially in the light of the planned economy although elements of market coordination have been gradually and partially introduced. This is the reality that the study is facing and also an existing premise that was not addressed in the descriptions and analyses in previous chapters. The clear-cut declaration was made by the 14th National Congress of the Communist Party of China and the 8th National People's Congress in 1993 that the target of the Chinese reform is to establish a socialist market economy. This significantly speeds up the process of the marketization of the Chinese economy.

Confronted with such a drastic change, it is impossible to sidestep a number of questions: how has the process of marketization affected or is affecting the poor people? How does the changing macroeconomic environment restrain the implementation of antipoverty programs? What countermeasures are expected to be taken to continue the process approaching the target of alleviating and eventually eliminating the poverty? To answer these questions, it is necessary to examine separately the reactions of government organs as well as the farmers towards the new institutional arrangements. It is because marketization not only directly alters the socioeconomic circumstances of the farmers but also affects, through government behaviors, the production and lives of rural families.

FOOD SECURITY

In the economic field, the reforms so far have promoted the agricultural development in poor regions, especially food production. The rate of self-sufficiency in foodgrain in poor regions increased from 60 percent at the end of the 1970s to 70 percent at the beginning of the 1990s (Jiang Zhongyi 1992), showing a significant improvement in food security for the poor people. This indicates a special feature of the Chinese reform, which differs from the practice of the marketization in the former Soviet Union and some eastern European countries, where no sooner had the institutional changes begun than have the food shortages brought to the ordinary people the threat of existence. An important reason for this difference, besides the lower degree of urbanization in China and the less dependence of most of the Chinese on the market for food consumption, lies in the fact that the Chinese government has never taken the policy of "laissez faire" during the process of marketization, while the alleviation of food shortages has been the result of farming input increases made simultaneously by the government and farmers.

The substitution of family farming for collective management was the institutional factor pushing the growth in agricultural production during the 1980s. It helped every farmer in the country to obtain the usufruct right on a plot of farmland thus enabling the farmers to be consciously responsible of the food security for their respective families. For poor households, their meager cash income combined with the price instability at the foodgrain market had compelled them to increase foodgrain yield by all means so as to meet the needs of their families, which was in line with the interests of the local governments. In the reform of foodgrain purchase and marketing system, the Central Government gradually reduced subsidies to the provinces which are not foodgrain buyers for transportation, storage, and marketing of foodgrain, thus transferring part of the financial burdens to local governments. Countermeasures taken by the developed provinces, Guangdong, for example, are mainly the decrease or even abolition of the subsidies while importing foodgrain from outside. However, for less-developed provinces, restrained by financial difficulties, they had no other choice but to further strengthen their own foodgrain production and raise the level of self-sufficiency. On the part of the Central Government, though subsidies on foodgrain marketing was decreased, its responsibilities in the promotion of foodgrain production and diversification of agricultural in poor regions were not shirked, because food security had long been deemed as a necessity in the maintenance of social stability.

It was exactly the unanimity of the three parties mentioned above in their aims and common efforts to promote new technics and made additional farming inputs that led to a higher rate of foodgrain self-sufficiency in the poor regions. The "project for sufficient food and clothing" (Wenbao-Gongcheng in Chinese alphabetic terms) organized by the Ministry of Agriculture during the late 1980s gives a proof on this point. The content of this "Wenbao-Gongcheng" was the extension of the hybrid maize growing technic of "plastic film covered cultivation" in the poor counties of 17 midwestern provinces (The Ministry of Agriculture and others 1987). Besides the arrangement of specific loan with subsidized interest for this project, the Central Government also allotted necessary materials every year at par. In 1989, and for one item of the project only covering an area of 10 million mu, 220,000 tons of chemical fertilizers and 30,000 tons of plastic films were allotted at par (The State Council Leading Group for the Development of Poor Areas 1989). The Ministry of Agriculture and the local governments also mobilized the departments in charge of technical extension to conduct technical training courses, to help the poor households buying improved varieties, farming chemicals, plastic films, chemical fertilizers and other means of production, and to give technical advice in fields. The extension of this maize-growing technology increased the yield by at least 100 kilograms of maize every mu and effectively eased the food shortage problem of the 15 million people in the mountainous areas (Yang Zhong 1993). This result coincides with the conclusion of the authors' nutrition analysis based on the sample studies (see Chapter 7.2).

The discussions above explained only the effects of government intervention leaving the impact of marketization on food security of the poor not yet involved. During the 1980s, when the government was gradually loosening its control over prices, the costs of both the agricultural input goods and farm products showed a tendency of going up, raising 57.7 percent and 64.2 percent, respectively, from the year 1985 to 1990 (State Statistical Bureau 1991). However, due to the low commercialization rate of farm products of rural households in poor regions, benefits earned by the farmers through price rising of farm products usually failed to compensate for the losses they suffered from the price hikes of the input. Furthermore, the main products of the rural households were foodgrain, while the inputs mostly used were chemical fertilizers, pesticides, and plastic films. During the period from 1985 to 1989, the retail price of foodgrain increased 80 percent, while the price of these inputs were more than doubled (Policy Division of the Ministry of Agriculture 1992). Thus, it can be conceived that without the producer subsidies, it would be difficult for the poor households to increase their inputs for foodgrain production and would be thus impossible to improve their food security on the basis of the plot of land they respectively managed.

According to the theory of the formation of market prices, price subsidies lead distortion to the price signals, which will finally impair the efficiency in the disposal of resources. Moreover, under circumstances of co-existing multiple price systems, the practice of subsidies usually provide organs in charge of marketing and distribution of commodities with conveniences for rent seeking activities and to hold back funds originally for the purpose of assisting poor households. Presently, the reform in the system of input goods supply tends to end this state of co-existence of multiple price systems and to put into effect the practice of pricing different commodities sheerly according to their respective demand and supply conditions on the market. Some institutions for poverty alleviation and government officials in poor regions widely think that this will enhance the cost of poverty alleviation programs and weaken the effects of preferential policies. But, as a matter of fact, an immediate advantage of the single price system will show that it diminishes the leakages of the poverty alleviation funds in the course of their transmissions. Presupposing that the government provides poor households, especially those in dire poverty, with technical and fiscal supports through other channels, the abolition of the system of supplying goods and materials at par prices through the administrative channel would bring about more advantages than drawbacks for the poor people.

Most of the farmland in poor regions are barren and unproductive and can only be counted as marginal land. Theoretically, if the government could help the fertile agricultural areas to further increase their production while making nonfarming investment in the poor regions, the comparative advantages of regional trade might be greater. Unfortunately, the poor regions have no favorable environments for nonagricultural development. Under the circumstance of existing socioeconomic structure, the government cannot but take the choice of strengthening the self-sufficient small-scale farming as the recipe for easing the problem of food shortages of the rural poor.

POSSIBILITIES OF INCREASE
IN NONAGRICULTURAL EMPLOYMENT

In spite of the difficulties in developing nonfarming economies in poor regions, the Central Government still set up a special credit program to support the establishment of county and township enterprises. The number of people employed in rural enterprises in the 120 most poor counties of the nation amounted to 4 percent of the overall rural labor force, while the national average of the same index was 22.1 percent (World Bank 1992b). Thus, it is evident that trying to solve the problem of employment in poor regions through rural enterprises is just like trying to put out a burning cartload of fuel with a cup of water (a traditional Chinese description for utterly inadequate measures). What is to be worried about more is that most of the enterprises are suffering from the problem of high production costs and heavy losses thereby becoming insolvent big debtors of the banks and bottomless pits absorbing continuously government financial subsidies. It can be predicted that with the establishment of the market economy and the formation of the unified national market, such enterprises can hardly survive the competition. However, the results will not bear directly and seriously upon the poor. It is because that these enterprises have not truly created many jobs at all and even less to the poor. During the surveys, the authors found that in these government-erected enterprises, persons having petticoat influences with officials were first employed. It is thus obvious that whether to maintain such enterprises or to let them close down, the biggest losers would be the government revenues and the banks. Such waste and misuse of resources would finally do harm to the opportunities of the poor households to obtain loans for their economic development because existing funds are very limited after all.

It is not that the authors stand against the development of rural enterprises in poor regions, but that the authors would like to point out frankly the necessity of pushing forward the reforms of enterprises. Running enterprises in poor regions in the traditional pattern of planned economy will bring them into the same predicament that the large and medium-size state enterprises are presently facing. Nonfarming industries in poor regions are still in their initial stage of development. As a plain paper, it is now easier for people to design on it development formulas different from those traditional models. On the one aspect, existing enterprises must get out of the swaddling clothes of the government and go bravely into the market, therein improving their management and striving for existence amid competition. On the other hand, the government should take measures to encourage the private initiatives and promote the establishment and development of non-public enterprises.

To bring the idea into effect, it needs not only funds but also qualified technical and managerial personnel. The problem lies in the fact that both of these two factors flow incessantly towards the developed areas during the process of marketization. It was estimated that funds flowing from the less-developed provinces to the developed coastal areas, through such channels as stock transactions, bonds, lottery tickets, interbank lending, and others, amounted to several tens of billion RMB yuan in the year 1992 only. High-qualified laborers distributed to poor counties according to state plan before the reforms are now departing one after another. In some of the counties, only one or two university graduates of the 1970s still remain (Gao Hongbin 1993). Factors flowing towards areas with higher factor return is the inevitable outcome of the resource allocation through market. Otherwise, there would be no improvement in allocative efficiency to talk about. It is then inconceivable that the factors should move against this trend without government intervention.

The government allotment of funds for poverty alleviation is not for the purpose of seeking high efficiencies, but intends to maintain social equity, taking it as a measure for rectification of market failure. In a complete planned economy, once a fund enters a certain area, it would not be able to move out. Under the present circumstance of a partial market economy, the banks have the conveniences of transferring funds to the developed areas and making profits from the price differentials of funds contained in the credits with interest subsidies given by the Central Government for poverty alleviation purpose (Liu Yunjiu and Qiu Fangji 1993). Thus, the capital mobility brought about by the marketization has made the poor households more difficult to get loans in their need, while the local financial institutions are gaining more benefits. To confront this situation and safeguard the interests of the poor, besides the establishment of independent institutions to supervise the conduct of the banks, it is desirable to encourage farmers to set up self-help groups and cooperative financial organizations so as to strengthen their bargaining positions vis-à-vis the banks.

The development prospect of enterprises in poor regions and the direction of flow of scarce factors indicate that during a considerably long period of time, henceforth, the migration of labor towards areas with rapid economic growth will remain an important way to increase the employment and income of the poor. This conclusion goes in conformity with the remarks made by a World Bank mission on the issue of employment in Chinese poor regions (World Bank 1992b). It is not that all people hunting for jobs can find work. Employment opportunities provided by cities and developed areas are far from enough to absorb the migrating labor. It is estimated that the number of the labor in need of jobs for the next decade amounts to 280 million people, of which about 68 million will be from the urban areas, while around 210 million from the rural (*Fu Jian Daily* Office 1993a). Moreover, the China Association of Labor Force estimated in 1992 that there are presently about 80 million surplus labor in Chinese countryside and about 10 million are migrating around every year, seeking employment, with about 20 to 30 percent of the 10 million failing to find any work (Jiang Zhongyi 1993). It would not be surprising if only the percentages were taken into consideration. But if the absolute number of the losers in the job hunting competition are examined, it would be amazing enough that it should be equivalent to the population of a European metropolis. What is also noteworthy is that the absorption of nonnative labor by the rural enterprises in developed areas remain subject to the restriction of the village community barriers. The village community ownership of enterprises automatically calls into existence the exclusion of permanent migrants. The reason for this lies in the fact that once a nonnative employee becomes a local villager, he (or she) will have the right of sharing the capital returns of the village community. Under such a background, rural enterprises having hold of their grounds in domestic market are tending to replace the labor-intensive technics with capital intensive technics that lead to the gradual decrease of job opportunities created by new investment.

Besides the factor of limitation of demand, the laborers from poor regions, on the part of the supply in labor market, are weak in the competition due to their lower educational and physical standards. Most of the migrants are presently from the medium-developed provinces and have become forceful competitors in the market of unskilled labor. This does not mean that the laborers from poor regions will surely be the losers in the competition. Statistics in the sample survey of this research indicate that those working or in business outside make up about 20 percent of the total laborers and most of them are with 8-12 years of schooling, which is considered a higher educational level in present rural China. It shows that even though it is not desirable to be optimistic about the prospects of increasing the employment and income of the poor through labor migration, yet if the investments in human resource in poor regions are increased, there do exist the possibility of granting them more opportunities.

RURAL SOCIAL SERVICES

Speaking of the investments in manpower resources, we will focus our discussions hereby on the closely related issue of changes in the education and health care sectors during the course of marketization. This is because the services they provide, together with food security, play the decisive role in the existence and development of the poor people. A number of studies home and abroad have proved that the improvement of education and health services helps the control of population growth, the lessening of environment pressure, and, finally, the alleviation and even the elimination of poverty (Getubig and Shams 1991). For the convenience of explanation, the author figures a schematic drawing to show the relationship between the current economic activities of the poor and the sectors concerning food production, sanitation, health protection, and education (Figure 9.1). As a matter of fact, discussions in this chapter will be set off in line with the logic embodied in Figure 9.1.

Figure 9.1—Flow of investments in human resources of the poor population

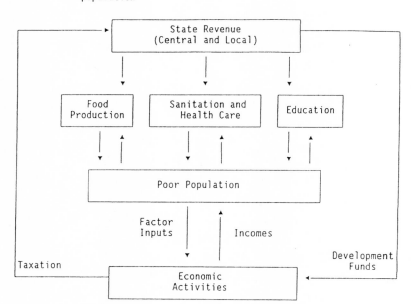

A number of foreign scholars, after making comparisons between indices of average life expectancy of human beings, death rate of children below 5 years old, ratio between population and number of medical personnel, rate of illiteracies and others, hold that there existed indications of retrogression in Chinese rural social services (Drèze and Sen 1989). Whether correct or not in this conclusion, it serves more than an alarm for the market-oriented Chinese economic reforms. A World Bank expert group, in its investigation report on Chinese poor regions, broadly discussed the changes in social services during recent more than 10 years and put forward a conclusion closer to reality that said that there were essential improvement in social services during the 1980s but those most benefitting from it were urban inhabitants and the middle-upper income groups in the countryside. The situation of high rate of illiteracy and malnutrition among the absolute poor remained roughly in the similar state as in the end of the 1970s (World Bank 1992b). It means that differences between urban and rural areas and among various regions and individuals are enlarging not only in the aspect of income but also in social services.

It is not that few people at the decisionmaking level know the importance of education to the development of human resources and the growth of the whole national economy. There has been no lack of persons of deep insight at the National Congresses in recent years going around campaigning for increases in educational investment. The data announced by the State Statistics Bureau also shows that the yearly educational expenditure of the state has always been on the increase. But the changes in the ratio of yearly educational expenditure in overall state financial expenditure show a shape of reverse "U," increasing from 12 percent in 1980 to 16.4 percent in 1988 (State Statistical Bureau 1991) and falling back to the level of the early 1980s again by the year 1992 (Liu Zhongli 1993). Moreover, the increase of investment is not necessarily leading to the enhancement of the educational level of all people. There are nearly 200 million illiteracies in China at present, equivalent to one among every four the world over. During the period from 1980 to 1988, more than 37 million students dropped out of middle and primary schools all over the country, with most of the study discontinuance cases happening in rural areas. Of the more than 4 million students dropping out of schools every year, one-fourth had stopped their studies due to the poorness of their families. The sample survey of the authors showed that the rate of illiteracy in the 7-15 year old age group reached 25.7 percent, 1.3 percentage points higher than the 24.4 percent in the 15-45 year old age group, offering a proof of the intensified problem in poor regions of children being deprived of their schooling opportunities. Although the "Project of Hope" raised by the Chinese Youth and Children Development Fund has been financing schooling, every year since 1989, for 100,000 children in poor regions, it is, of course, difficult for the project to solve the schooling problem of all the remaining poor children, totaling nearly 1 million every year, who failed to attend school at their school ages (Huang Chuanhui 1993).

Reasons for the sharp contrast between the increasing educational investment and the worsening situation in rural education are very complicated. First of all, it reflects the "urban bias" in the field of education manifesting in the uneven distribution of investment between towns and countryside as well as between high and primary education. Secondly, the local educational expenditures are nowadays borne mainly by the local governments, since, after the reform of financial systems, so that in provinces and counties where the local revenues fall short of expenditures, there would be serious insufficiencies in the rural educational funds that have been endangering the normal operation of the schools with cases of defaults in the payment of teachers' salaries and delays in the repair of dangerous school houses existing here and there. Thus, it becomes difficult not only to maintain the normal standard of teaching equalities but even to stabilize the ranks of school teachers. As the market has been offering other job opportunities with higher remunerations, the running off of teachers are as serious as the discontinuation of studies on the part of the students. It was reported for the year 1992 that about 450,000 teachers all over the country changed their profession (*Fu Jian Daily* Office 1993b). Furthermore, existing education in the Chinese countryside is mainly an academically-oriented general education lacking of vocational schools with quicker returns. Rural families, even with higher incomes, usually prefer sending their sons and daughters to work at an early date rather than to finance them studying in general middle schools, unless they find their children hopeful of being enrolled in high schools in the future (Zhu Ling 1991). In poor regions, it is not only the above-mentioned reasons, but exactly the poverty that has deprived the children of their educational opportunities. It is because of poorness that their families are incapable of paying the tuitions, even though the tuitions charged by schools in poor areas are much lower than the national average, about 20 to 25 yuan for every student and every school term. This also indicates that it is almost impossible to carry out the nine-year compulsory education in the poor regions in the near future. Only for the realization of the target of "education for everybody in 2000," it needs the government to provide stipends for the poor children's primary school courses. To rely simply on private donations is far from enough.

The changes in the sector of sanitation and health care are more or less the same as in the education sector. In the background of improvement in national average level, medical services in the countryside failed to show essential betterment. Only to compare the condition of equipment between urban and rural hospitals, the above judgment can be rightly confirmed (Table 9.1). However, compared with the national average, the situation in poor regions are even worse. An investigation made by the Ministry of Health in 1989 on the situation in medical service in 300 poor counties showed that the infantile death rate reached an average of 68 cases per 1,000 and maternal mortality was as high as 202 cases per 100,000, 50 percent and 200 percent higher than the national average, respectively. Most of the infantile and maternal mortality cases were due to the delay in treatment. And the relative decrease of public health expenditures and the decline in the rural cooperative system of medical treatment were explained as the direct reasons for the phenomenon (World Bank 1992b).

Unlike the education system, the system of cooperative medical treatment in the countryside had been closely connected with the system of People's Communes. Although the system of contracted farming has been substituted for the Commune's function of organizing production, it can not exercise the function of controlling and financing the medical affairs at the grass-roots level. During the 1980s, when the production system in the countryside was

Table 9.1—Average number of beds and health technicians in every hospital

Classification of Hospitals	1985 Beds	1985 Health Technicians	1989 Beds	1989 Health Technicians	1990 Beds	1990 Health Technicians
National total of all kinds	37.3	39.6	41.5	43.2	42.0	44.2
Hospitals at and above county level	129.4	134.5	135.6	140.8	136.9	143.0
Township medical centers	15.2	16.5	15.2	16.1	15.1	16.3
Others	29.4	45.5	42.2	41.7	44.5	42.6

Source: State Statistical Bureau, *The Chinese Yearbook of Statistics 1991* (Beijing: Chinese Statistics Publishing House, 1991), 773.

changing and village primary schools still retained the nature as a public
entity, the medical rooms at the village level took the lead in carrying out the
system of individual management. Thus, with the weakening of the public
nature of the medical service network at the rural grass-roots level, the voice
calling for government financial support for rural medical services inevitably lowered down as well. In addition, now that the charges for medical
treatments are to be paid by farmers themselves and the poor usually cannot
afford to make the payments, the quality of the rural medical service tends
to deteriorate.

Besides, the medical industry has entered the market, a sellers' market,
due to the existence of monopolies. The multifold increase of medical costs
in recent years has intensified the farmers' difficulties in medical treatment.
Investigations show that 20 percent of the patients in the countryside failed
to have timely treatment because of their incapability of paying the charges.
For the same reason, 68 percent of the patients who should be hospitalized
failed to be in hospital (Feng Tongqiang and Feng Zhaodi 1993).

Due to financial reforms in the medical and health sector, the share of
service receipts in the total financial sources of the sector has been increasing, while the government appropriations, though on the increase every year
in its absolute amount, has shown a downward tendency in its percentage in
the overall government expenditures. The situation has affected mostly the
rural institutions of public sanitation, maternal and infantile health care, and
epidemic prevention, resulting in the low efficiency of these set-ups and the
renewed rampancy of the epidemic and local diseases that had previously
been under control. Against this background, the Ministry of Health started,
since 1991, a nationwide program to renovate the health centers at the township level and the epidemic prevention stations and maternal and infantile
health protection stations at the county level. Relevant investment are made
jointly by all sides concerned. Due to financial difficulties in poor regions,
some of the counties have introduced into this field the funds originally allotted for "Yigong-daizhen" (to provide work as a form of relief) projects so
as to meet their pressing needs.

The problems in the fields of rural education and health care as described
above should not be simplified as failures of reform or totally the outcomes

of marketization. As a matter of fact, the phenomenon has been developed due to many factors.

First, the "urban bias" in the disposition of resources in these two sectors has been in existence even before the reforms. And during the reforms, the rural social organizations originally in existence had been abolished at a time when the new ones were not yet built up fully, thus weakening immensely the efforts of the countryside vis-à-vis the cities striving for public resources and leading to the further intensification of the bias instead of rectification. For example, the system of free medical service has been, from the very beginning, a privilege of urban population (the employees of the state-owned enterprises and institutions), which is not accessible to farmers and their families, who make up the great majority of the whole population of the country. In contrast with the situation in the rural medical and health services, where public expenditure decreased remarkably following the decline of the system of cooperative medical treatment, the government expenditure in the free medical service system increased tremendously, along with the rising prices of the service. The reason for this lies in the fact that the system of the service remains unchanged even during the reforms. Now, the government expenditure for this service stands at 4,000 million yuan RMB every year, constituting one-fourth of the overall medical and health expenditures of the state (Feng Tongqiang and Feng Zhaodi 1993), while the number of persons enjoying the benefits of the service lies below 100 million, less than one-eleventh of the nationwide population. It shows an unequal pattern of distribution of resources.

Second, the Chinese economy has looked so far as a government operated machine which the preference of the high level decisionmakers can master the disposal of resources. Since the 1980s, the tendency of pursuing high-speed economic growth at the government decisionmaking level has caused the flow of more public investment towards the sectors of direct production, symbolized by the periodic overheating in making investment and the excessive expansion in the scale of capital construction. Unlike the investment in production, investment in social services such as in education and health undertakings do not show up their benefits immediately, but through the long course of economic development, indirectly and gradually.

Thus, while governments at different levels are concentrating their attention in the immediate results of high-speed growth, the sectors of social service would naturally be elbowed to the last position in the sequence of distribution of resources. In the poverty alleviation programs, the situation in the disposition of resources has been the same as such. Therefore, one can come to the idea that the bias in the decisionmaking of the government is an important reason leading to the depressing state in the education and health services in countryside and poor regions.

Third, the myth of market has to a certain extent induced the reforms in the education and health care service systems. The commodity nature of the services was explicitly emphasized and raise of the service prices has been increasingly relied upon as a means to solve their financial difficulties. Due to the low payment capacity on the part of the population in poor regions, the shrinkage in the supply of education as well as health and medical services thereby came to arise. It can be predicted that without government intervention, the conditions of social services for the poor population will be even worse.

The discussion here does not mean that the private suppliers and market competition should be excluded from the sector of public services but tends to indicate the fact that during the economic reforms, the improvement of social services has been lagging far behind the economic growth and failed to ensure the basic requirements of women and children among the weak crowds, especially the poor population due to the meagerness of the institutional construction in this field. The target of eliminating absolute poverty should not contain only the food security area, but, also, as contents of the same importance, the insurance of elementary education as well as the sanitation and health services covering all poor population, because it is exactly the latter that guarantees that this crowd of people will never return to poverty again after having gotten rid of it (World Bank 1993). Taking this point into consideration, the Central Government should also carry out policies preferential towards poor regions when making education investment as well as investment in the field of health and sanitation.

In fact, even in some developed countries of market economy in Europe and America, the education and health undertakings are not regulated freely through the market. Instead, "dual track" or "three-track" systems are established to meet the requirements of various groups with different incomes. Taking Great Britain as an example, there exist both private and public schools and hospitals. The existence of different suppliers facilitates the improvement of quality of services through competitions. However, it is exactly the public institutions that have ensured the most basic services for the low-income strata. In terms of the charge collection systems in medical services of many countries the highest income strata of the society usually pay the expenses fully by themselves, while the government free medical services are only for the weak crowds, with the remainder to be covered by the social medical insurance system (partly paid by the patients themselves). Although there exists no lack of critics against such systems, in comparison with the current situation in China, where the poor discordantly pay more for the service, it cannot but be considered as a kind of more reasonable and feasible institutional arrangement. Moreover, when governments at various levels are all confronted with financial difficulties and there exists a massive amount of poor population, it would be nothing but wishful thinking to raise excessively high expectation on the standard of services supplied under poverty alleviation programs.

MACRO-ECONOMIC CONSTRAINTS ON POVERTY ERADICATION SCHEMES

Analysis on prospects of basic needs securities, employment and income of poor population shows that to get rid of poverty, development aids are not only needed, but also, eagerly, a safety net (that is, a social security system including reliefs, insurance, and welfare), to resist different kinds of attacks arising from marketization. A stable and continuous economic growth combined with an equal distribution of social securities can be regarded as the ideal state of development. However, both the institutional construction and the supply of development aids need a huge amount of funds so that the macroeconomic, especially the state financial, constraints on the poverty alleviation programs must be considered. It is also because the poverty alleviation programs in China have been from the beginning and will be to the very end mainly a kind of public action supported by overwhelmingly public resources.

Since 1985, the absolute poor in China has decreased from 125 million to 80 million people (Yang Zhong 1993). Those remaining in poverty are now inhabiting mainly in areas with the worst natural conditions and poorest resources, where the elimination of poverty still needs prolonged public actions. During the last eight years, the yearly financial inputs in poor regions, including loans on favorable terms, financial appropriations, and poverty alleviation funds from different central functionary departments were estimated at about 10 billion yuan totally (Wang Xinhuai 1993). Funds, as such, were mainly economic aid while the improvement of social services needs much more additional investment. According to World Bank specialists, the implementation of the special programs of education and health, which will enable the 15 million poor children to fulfill the six-year primary school education and decrease the maternal and infantile death rates among the poor by one-third, needs at least a yearly expense of 2 billion yuan (World Bank 1992b). The figures may help people get a rough idea about the high density of monetary inputs necessary for the poverty alleviation programs.

However, judging from the current macroeconomic situation in China and the financial conditions of the state, the possibility of further expansion of poverty alleviation funds is rather limited. After the 1989-91 economic retrenchment, a new round of heats in the pursuance of high-speed growth has once again landed the state financially in a predicament. The financial deficit of the Central Government reached as high as more than 20 billion yuan in the year of 1992, while local budgets, though in a balance when being drawn up, appeared in an overall deficit during their implementation, amounting to more than 3 billion yuan (Liu Zhongli 1993). It can be predicted according to past experience, that without the staging of new measures of institutional reform such a state of affairs cannot be changed fundamentally.

The primary reason for such a financial deficit lies in the overheat of investment driven by the government. While the decentralization-oriented institutional reforms in the financial sector weakened the macro-regulation capacity of the central finance, the position of local governments at different levels as the main bodies of investment remained unchanged. Thus, for officials who assume no risk, but can enjoy the benefits, the expansion of the competence of local governments further encouraged their excitements in making investments. Due to the fact that existing enterprises have become independent economic entities, officials responsible for investment usually show little interest in the reforms and innovation of the enterprises, while being enthusiastic in setting up new projects. Taking public investment in the year of 1992 as an example, the expenditures of many local governments in capital construction increased by more than 30 percent. The pressure of monetary shortages and inflation arising therefrom has been keenly acknowledged by all Chinese people.

The second big category of expenditure causing the financial strains has been government subsidies, which made up near one-third of the total state expenditure in the year 1990 (State Statistical Bureau 1991). About 40 percent of the subsidies are price allowances used mainly to partly compensate the losses of urban inhabitants due to the rising of prices of daily necessities. This category of subsidies can be counted as a policy expenditure because it has been used by the government as a measure to reduce the resistance in price reforms. The greater part of the subsidies was used to compensate the losses of the enterprises, the background of which lies in the fact that about two-thirds of the state enterprises has long been in a state of losses so that, as representative of the state and owner of the enterprises, the government bears the responsibility of maintaining, through subsidies, their existence.

A related problem hereon is the drain on state revenue. Now that the greater part of state enterprises are in a state of low efficiency, it is impossible for the government to expect abundant receipts from them in support of state revenues. Meanwhile, the nonstate enterprises are still in their newborn stage, not yet grown up enough to become the main force backing government finance. Their contributions to the state revenue amounted to only one-third as much as those made by state enterprises (State Statistical Bureau 1991). Furthermore, due to the fact that the taxation system in China has not yet been well-organized, there exist many outflows from state incomes. This can be observed through the reverse increases in some of the main components of state financial sources against the state of affairs in taxation. During the period from January to May in 1993, the sale of commodities by collective enterprises in terms of production values increased by 55.6 percent, while the income tax paid by these enterprises reduced by 10.7 percent. In the same period, profits of state industrial enterprises increased 1.9-fold, while the income tax and regulation tax they paid, together with the profits they handed in, decreased by 30.1 percent (Liu Zhongli 1993). To cope with such a grave financial situation, the long-term strategy would be the comprehensive reforms in the fields of property rights, investments, money and banking, revenue and taxation, enterprises, and price systems, while the immediate measures within the reach of the government are those to increase sources of the revenue and reduce expenditures. But the expenditures having effects on social stabilities can hardly be cut, such as those for national defense, public securities, and government establishments strengthening the regime, while some others directly involving the individual benefits can neither be immediately reduced or even abolished, such as the subsidies. Thus, the sector of social services (including education, health, and scientific research), which has been in weaker bargaining positions in the distribution of financial resources, may come to bear the brunt of the retrenching measures. Against this background, expectations of improvement in social services in poor areas cannot but recede accordingly.

Even if the existing density of inputs of poverty alleviation funds is maintained, it is still necessary to predict the possibility of increase in poor people. First of all, the newborn poor would be the urban poor which are closely related to the reforms in the enterprises as well as in the systems of employment and wages. Now that the state budget has been seriously overburdened with the subsidies for state enterprises, it becomes a must to push these enterprises to go to the market. However, if it is the market that makes the choice, the enterprises with low efficiencies and heavy losses will finally go bankrupt, thus generating, unavoidably, millions of unemployed. In such a case, even if the systems of unemployment insurance were arranged, there would still be families falling economically down to the level below the poverty line. Second, among the newborn poor, there may appear class-based poverty arising from the unequal distribution of properties. Now that diversified property ownership has appeared in the course of marketization and incomes from property are entering on an increasingly enlarged scale, the field of individual income distribution, the emergence of the class-based poverty logically becomes a certainty. Therefore, the poverty during the transition period of socioeconomic systems will no more be confined in the scope of the rural poor and it has become a must for the future antipoverty schemes to include the content of urban poverty alleviation.

The discussions above show that the carrying out of antipoverty schemes is closely related to the improvement of macroeconomic environment. The realization of the latter not only ensures the collection of funds for the former but will finally lead to decreases in the incidence of poverty. The course of improvement in macroeconomy itself means the development of sectional reforms into a comprehensive reform that may inevitably lead to the heightening of the rate of poverty. Furthermore, the newly added financial requirements, because of the expansion in the areas of reform, may further restrain the supply of funds for antipoverty schemes. For example, to push the state enterprises entering the market, establishment of a social security system running abreast with the progress of market economy is absolutely necessary, which, in turn, needs the backing of tremendous financial inputs.

Although it is really something of a dilemma to push forward the comprehensive reforms and to reduce poverty, yet for the sake of eliminating poverty from its roots, the choice can only be the further promotion of the reforms. Based upon this premise, the poverty in China cannot be a problem to be solved in several years. Instead, the antipoverty schemes will be prolonged and transcentury public actions.

10

✳✳✳✳✳✳✳✳✳✳✳✳✳✳
SUMMARY
✳✳✳✳✳✳✳✳✳✳✳✳✳✳

U nder the background of economic reform and large-scale antipoverty activities in China and by means of empirical research, this study has identified the role of the Yigong-daizhen program in poverty alleviations through the examination of its impact on employment, income, and nutrition status of the rural households in poor areas.

The problems of poverty in China at present are mainly regional ones in the rural sector. The economic reform begun since the end of the 1970s had energetically promoted the growth of the rural economy and raised the income level of farmers as a whole during a short period, thus rapidly changing the situation of commonly existed poorness in the Chinese countryside and extricating nearly 200 million people from the state of absolute poverty. The changes not only have helped the Chinese Government to concentrate its efforts to solve the remaining poverty problems, but also have facilitated the identification of the poor still in existence. These existed by then still a rural population totaling about one-tenth of the national gross and living in areas with poor resources and fragile infrastructure, who had scarcely benefited from the reforms and were still under the menace of food shortage. It was exactly because of this that the Chinese Government set a poverty line in 1985, a per capita yearly net income of less than 200 yuan, to discern the poor, on the basis of which nearly 700 counties were selected as the main target of poverty alleviation efforts. Since then, while striving for the progress of infrastructural construction in poor regions, measures were also taken to stimulate local governments and farmers, through the reforms in poverty alleviation policies, to tap their own potentials for economic development and extrication from poorness.

"Yigong-daizhen" is one of many poverty alleviation policies, the substance of which contains mainly government investments in kind in infrastructural construction of poor regions. It builds up material foundations for regional economic growth on the one hand and provides short-term job opportunities and income for the poor on the other. The projects thus raised are actually the same as the poverty alleviation programs internationally known as "public works." For the purpose of observation of the impact of Yigong-daizhen projects on different categories of poor regions and local rural households, the authors conducted case studies on road construction and drinking water supply projects in the provinces of Guizhou and Sichaun in 1990. Then they selected three poor counties, one for each of the three different categories of provinces¾the developed, the medium-developed, and the less-developed¾and made a sample survey in May and June of 1992. The counties thus selected were Linqu County of Shandong, Wangcang County of Sichuan, and Xiji County of Ningxia. The survey was made through questionnaires circulated on the two levels of village communities and rural households. At the level of village communities, the interviewees were leading members of the village committees.

Twelve administrative villages were selected from each of the three sample counties and were divided into three groups, with every four villages comprising one group. The first group consisted of villages participating in road projects and the second group, villages participating in drinking water supply projects, leaving the third one as a reference group not participating in any Yigong-daizhen projects. Household questionnaires were filled in on the basis of interviews with head of household couples, 10 from each of the villages selected through random samples. Data thus collected related to the conditions in the year of 1991. Due to traffic difficulties, only two villages were selected, instead of four, for the reference group of Wangcang County of Sichuan Province. However, 20 rural households were sampled in each of the two villages, instead of 10, so the number of villages sampled in the three counties totaled 34 and the number of sample rural households was 360.

Examination showed that 358 questionnaires were valid. Data obtained from the questionnaires were also supplemented by the *Yearbook of Statistics* and other information published by the State Statistics Bureau, as well as related materials provided by functional departments of the State Planning Commission, the Ministry of Finance, the Ministry of Communications, and the Ministry of Water Conservancy and Irrigation. Besides the statistical yearbooks and Yigong-daizhen working reports of the sample provinces and counties, historical literature on culture, geography, and economy of the three counties also made their contributions.

Existing literature shows that situations in the three surveyed areas are discrepant of one another naturally, socially, and economically; hence, the differences among their respective emphases in the course of carrying out the Yigong-daizhen policies. With its relatively strong economic strength and intensive financial aid, the provincial government of Shandong has made the Yigong-daizhen projects in the province approaching the level of regular capital constructions, thus becoming a means to bring the poor counties speeding up their economic growth and catching up the average standard of the province. The absolute number of poor population and the area of poor regions in Sichuan Province are all far greater than that in Shandong, hence the dual significance was given to Yigong-daizhen projects in the province. The projects serve not only the improvement of the living circumstance of the poor, but also the economic growth of the entire province. It is only in Ningxia, which characteristically is less-developed, that the Yigong-daizhen project truly bears the original meaning of its name, with relief being its main purpose. As far as the studied counties are concerned, the Yigong-daizhen program there has been merged together with local socioeconomic development plans. All local governments of the three counties have been using the projects to solve their major difficult problems of fragile infrastructure and poor social services at the village level, food shortages of the farmers, underemployment, and low income. Here, the policy of Yigong-daizhen has combined the three components of relief, growth, and development together.

Quite a number of developing countries take public works as a means for poverty alleviation. Compared with their organization patterns, the distinguishing feature of the Yigong-daizhen program in China lies in its targeting mechanism. The Chinese Government selects the beneficiaries through the adjustment of project sites and investment orientations. The central government has stipulated that the projects can be carried out only in poor regions, while, within the framework of the poor regions, it is the village communities (that is, the administrative villages), not the individuals and households and persons, that are to be targeted by the project. The principle of efficiency has been carried out by the county and township governments when making decisions on the establishment of the projects so as to ensure the success of the projects and the effectiveness of the investments. The village communities that are chosen for the projects usually have relatively favorable socioeconomic conditions. During the implementation of the projects, it is the village communities that are responsible for the mobilization of labor under the principle of equality¾equal opportunity for all households and individuals. The operational pattern of the projects combining regional targeting and labor mobilization through village community participation has taken account of both "efficiency" and "equity," thus enabling the poor to be finally the majority of the benefitted population. This has also been proved by the estimation of the possibility of rural household participation in the projects by means of the Probit Model. Further, the contents of the projects also facilitate the village communities to be the benefitted units. After their completion, the projects would assume the shape of either the village communities' public infrastructures (roads, for example), or the properties of the village communities (such as terraced fields constructed and soils improved), or others. So, it is obviously impossible to exclude the nonpoor from the beneficiaries of the projects.

Another special feature of the Yigong-daizhen projects, different from the public works of other countries, lies in the fact that about one-half of the labor inputs made by farmers in the poor regions of developed and medium-developed provinces are obligatory workdays. Such a practice presupposes two conditions: first, the recognition of the farmers' obligation to participate in public investment through labor accumulation and, second, an existing income of the farmers that is capable of meeting their basic requirements of subsistence. However, calculations on the income of sample households showed that the paid labor of the participants in all the project areas had led to the simultaneous increase in both family income and welfare in the same year. It was also found that through an analysis of the Gini coefficient that the distribution of project earnings had more or less intensified the inequality in the disposable income of households. The results were supported by the fact that the opportunity of farmers taking part in the projects were restricted by the volume of available resources, the localities of the projects, and the barriers among the village communities so that not all laborers were able to obtain this portion of income. For the part of the participants, because some of them had joined the projects with their own machines, consequently, their project earnings included not only the wages but also the rewards to the capital, hence resulting in a higher degree of uneven distribution of project earnings and the expansion of overall Gini coefficient. It was only because of the relatively small share of earnings in the overall disposable income that the impact had been very limited.

The gaps between the disposable income of households are determined, first of all, by the regional differences, while the conditions of village infrastructure as well as material capital, human capital, and the amount of applied modern agricultural inputs of the rural households are also decisive factors of the income. It means that the effect of the Yigong-daizhen policy also had its limits. It has created only one of the many essential conditions for poverty alleviation and elimination. The poor need help in all aspects of culture, education, health, and production. So, only by taking long-term and comprehensive measures of investments can the poverty be gradually and stably alleviated.

Since the Yigong-daizhen projects are effective in increasing income of the participants, they will surely have impact also on the family expenditures of households, including food consumption expenses. It is from this viewpoint that surveys were made on the consumption and nutrition conditions of sample households. Statistic analyses show that food consumption constitutes the biggest component of expenditure of sample households, which relies mainly on family farming products. This reflects exactly the feature of subsistence economy of sample households. During the research, a classic method of nutrition analysis and the Formula for Grading Desired Diet Pattern Points, worked out by the Chinese Academy of Preventive Medical Science, were introduced, by means of which comparisons on food consumption and caloric structure of sample households were made. It was thus discovered that the situation of general malnutrition remained in poor counties of less-developed provinces, while the nutrition intake of the poor in medium-developed and developed provinces had reached the level of national average, indicating that the problem of food shortages in these areas had been alleviated. Due to the fact that the rewards for farmers participating in Yigong-daizhen projects were paid in the form of "purchasing coupons," which could be used only for purchase of nonfood commodities, the earnings of farmers from the projects had no direct effect on the improvement of food consumption and nutrition conditions of their families. But the projects having thus been constructed did have their indirect effects. The improvement of infrastructure had been the priority of the Yigong-daizhen projects prior to the year 1991, but since that year, the investments were concentrated in farmland and water conservancy capital construction, which are advantageous to the higher output of land. The implementation of both kinds of projects will benefit the supply of farm products, hence, the possibility of improving the nutrition condition of rural households. However, the former ones are more useful to areas where the problem of food shortages have been fundamentally solved, but the traffic difficulties remain, while the latter kind of projects are more meaningful to arise where food security has not yet been available. To set the order of priority, it is the village committees and the local governments that are most qualified to speak. Meanwhile, the Central Government should be flexible in making regulations on the proportion of investment divisions among different projects.

Now, the problem is that Yigong-daizhen projects have been organized and operated in line with the pattern of a traditional planned economy, hence the defects of rigidity in planning work from higher levels downward and the separation at times from requirements of the local populace. Besides, new problems are also coming thick and fast, which includes the daily increasing number of sectors participating in the distribution of project resources, the more complicated organizational systems, the rapid expansion of investment gap, the downward trend of efficiency in resource utilizations, the extension of project areas to nonpoor regions, and others. Such defects, having cropped up under the planned economy, can only be uprooted through the reforms on the system. However, during the transitional period, it can only resort to both the long-term and short-term measures to correct the planning failures whenever it happens.

The success and defects in the implementation of the policy of Yigong-daizhen have sketched a miniature of the Chinese macroeconomy in the transitional state. To continuously carry out the antipoverty schemes with this policy included will be closely connected with the improvement of the macroeconomic environment in its entirety. Based on this understanding, the authors have extended the research to impact the process of marketization on the poor and to macro constraints on the antipoverty schemes in the future, and, within the framework of which, hereby stress the following points:

1. The introduction of the market mechanisms in the Chinese economic reform during the recent 10 years and more has inestimably played an active role in the rise of resource disposition efficiency and the promotion of economic growth. However, historical experiences of home and abroad have proved that there is also "market failure" and that economic growth does not necessarily mean social development. The alleviation of poverty and the enhancement of the life quality of all citizens still needs government interventions through income redistribution and public investments. The combination of a stable and continuous economic growth and an equal distribution of social securities means an ideal state of development.

2. The large-scale poverty alleviation activities have eased the problem of food shortages in poor regions, but the supply of primary education and health and sanitation services has not yet had significant improvement. Further, the prospects of the security of basic requirements of the poor as well as their employment and income are also not that bright during the process of marketization. So, the government should by no means take the policy of Laissez faire.

3. Estimating from the present macroeconomic situation and the financial conditions of the state, the possibility of further increase of the poverty alleviation funds is very limited. To get out of the financial predicament, the only way out is to turn the present partial reforms into a comprehensive reform. However, the newly added financial expenditures heretofore will surely intensify further the constraints on the supply of funds for antipoverty purposes. Even though the existing input density of poverty alleviation funds were maintained, there would still be the possible increase in the number of the poor, the characteristic of which lies in:

a. The newly added poor will be those in the cities closely related with the reforms on the systems of enterprises, employment, and wages; and

b. Due to the emergence of diversified property ownership, the return to assets have been entering the field of personal income distribution with ever increasing dimensions, so that the poverty of strata based on the unequal distribution of properties would possibly crop up among the newly added poor.

Therefore, the poverty during the transition period will be no more confined in the countryside and the antipoverty schemes in the future must contain another part dealing specifically with the urban poor.

****
APPENDIX

****

Table 1—Conversion indices per reference person per day[a]

Age	Intensity of Physical Activities	Male	Female	Age	Intensity of Physical Activities	Male	Female	Pregnant Woman	Mother with Breast-Feeding
0-		0.150	0.150	17-	Very light	1.000	0.875	0.958	1.208
1-		0.335	0.310		Light	1.083	0.958	1.042	1.292
2-		0.375	0.350		Average	1.250	1.125	1.208	1.458
3-		0.458	0.438		Heavy	1.417	1.250	1.333	1.583
4-		0.500	0.479		Very heavy	1.667	1.375		1.708
5-		0.563	0.542	45-	Very light	0.917	0.792		
6-		0.604	0.583		Light	1.000	0.875		
7-		0.667	0.625		Average	1.125	1.000		
8-		0.708	0.667		Heavy	1.250	1.125		
9-		0.750	0.708		Very heavy	1.375	1.250		
10-		0.792	0.750	60-	Very light	0.833	0.708		
11-		0.833	0.792		Light	0.917	0.792		
12-		0.875	0.833		Average	1.042	0.875		
13-		0.917	0.875		Heavy	1.167	1.000		
14-		0.958	0.917		Very heavy	1.292	1.125		
15-		1.000	0.958	70-	Very light	0.750	0.667		
	Light	1.167	1.125		Light	0.833	0.780		
	Average	1.292	1.250		Average	0.958	0.875		
16-		1.167	1.000		Heavy	1.083	1.000		
	Light	1.333	1.167	80-		0.667	0.583		
	Average	1.500	1.333						
	Heavy	1.167	1.500						

[a] The conversion indices were formulated by the Institute of Nutrition, Chinese Academy of Preventative Medical Science, October 7, 1991, Beijing.

Table 2—The formula for grading desired diet pattern points

Source of Calories (Food Varieties)	Optimal Composition of Calories	Grading Standards	Points (Total=100)	Maximum Points[a]
	(percent)			
Cereals, roots and stems of grains	60	0.5	30.0	40
Animal foods	14	2.5	35.0	40
Added oils and fats	9	1.0	9.0	10
Beans and bean products	5	2.5	12.5	15
Sugar	5	0.5	2.5	5
Nut oilseeds	2	0.5	1.0	5
Vegetables and fruits	5	2.0	10.0	15
Wines and beverages	0	0.0	0.0	0

Source: Chen Chunming, "The Food Consumption and Nutrition Conditions of Farmers in the Six Provinces and a Municipality," a research paper (Chinese Academy of Preventive Medical Science, Beijing, 1992).

[a] Maximum points means that the points of a certain kind of food will no longer increase when the calories provided by it have surpassed its share in the optimal composition of calories.

****
BIBLIOGRAPHY
****

Agricultural Policy Research Office of Sichuan Provincial Committee of the Communist Party. 1989. Studies on development strategies of hilly areas of Sichuan. Chengdu: Agricultural Policy Research Office.

Ahmed, R., and M. Hossain. 1990. *Developmental impact of rural infrastructure in Bangladesh*. Research Report 83. Washington, D.C.: International Food Policy Research Institute.

Braun, J. von, T. Teklu, and P. Webb. 1991. *Labor-intensive public works for food security experience in Africa*. Working Papers on Food Subsidies 6. Washington, D.C.: International Food Policy Research Institute.

Braun, J. von, H. Bouis, S. Kumar, and R. Pandya-Lorch. 1992. *Improving food security of the poor: Concept, policy, and programs*. Washington, D.C.: International Food Policy Research Institute.

CCCCP (The Central Committee of the Chinese Communist Party). 1984. The notification on helping the poor areas to accelerate changes in their situation. Beijing: People's Republic of China.

_____. 1985a. Document No. 1. Beijing: People's Republic of China.

_____. 1985b. Document No. 19. Beijing: People's Republic of China.

Chen Chunming. 1992. The food consumption and nutrition conditions of farmers in the six provinces and a municipality. Research paper. Chinese Academy of Preventive Medical Science, Beijing.

Chen, Junsheng. 1991. The speech at the National Conference of Exchanging Experiences on Economic Development in Poor Mountainous Regions. 16 October.

Chen, Junshi, and Others. 1991. *The diet, lifestyle, and death rate in China*. China: The Publishing House of People's Health; Britain: Oxford University; U.S.A.: Cornell University.

Doldon, P. J., and G. H. Makepeace. 1987. *Interpreting sample selection effects*. Economics Letters 24. Elsevier Science Publisher B.V. (North-Holland).

DrPze, J., and A. Sen. 1989. *Hunger and public action*. Oxford: Clarendon Press.

Du, Runsheng. 1986. To explore the inherent vigour of the poor and change the features of the poor areas. *Journal of National Solidarity* 10, Beijing.

Fei, Xiaotong, and Others. 1988. *A study on the regional development planning and strategies*. Beijing: Zhanwang.

Feng, T., and Zhaodi Feng. 1993. Puzzles of medical services in the market economy. *Chinese Health Economy* 8.

Fields, G. 1980. *Poverty, inequality, and development*. Cambridge: Cambridge University Press.

Fu Jian Daily Office. 1993a. Employment pressure of the Chinese laborers. *Weekly Digest*, 3 November, Fuzhou.

_____. 1993b. The biggest difficulties of the primary education in the recent decade. *Weekly Digest*, 27 October, Fuzhou.

Gao, Hongbin. 1993. A speech at the National Conference of the Directors of Provincial Offices for Poverty Alleviation, 21 April, Beijing.

Gao, Xiaosu, and Zhao Jie. 1989. Investigation on temporary migrants in Beijing. Research Report. Beijing.

Getubig, I. P., and M. K. Shams. 1991. *Improving the design, management, and implementation of poverty alleviation programs*. Kuala Lumpur, Malaysia: Asian and Pacific Development Centre.

Greene, W. H. 1992. *LIMDEP Version 6.0, User's Manual and Reference Guide*. Australia: Econometric Software, Inc.

Guo, Fansheng. 1988. *Poverty and development.* Hangzhou: Zhejiang People's Publishing House.

Hartung, J., and B. Elpelt. 1986. *Multivariate Statistik.* Munich: R. Oldenbourg Verlag.

Hou, Jianmin. 1990. Benefit analysis and supervision of poverty alleviation projects. *Forum of Development* 9, Beijing.

Hu, Xianzhong. 1993. On current crisis of qualified personnel in China. *Xinhua Digest* 8.

Huang, Chuanhui. 1993. Facts in the "Hope Projects." *Xinhua Digest* 6.

Hydroelectricity Bureau of Qingchuan County. 1990. The report about the performance of the drinking water supply program.

Institute of Nutrition of the Chinese Academy of Preventive Medical Science. 1991. *The table of food components.* Beijing: People's Health Publishing House.

Institute of Population Research, Chinese Academy of Social Sciences. 1987. *The yearbook of Chinese population.* Beijing: Economic Management Publishing House.

_____. 1988. *The population yearbook of China.* Beijing: Economic Management Publishing House.

Institute of Rural Development, Chinese Academy of Social Sciences. 1991. The effects of the quality of grassroots cadres in poor regions to the economic development. Research Report. Beijing.

Jiang, Zhongyi. 1992. A research paper on the provision of foodgrains. A paper for reference. Beijing.

Jiang, Zhongyi. 1993. Policy suggests for the construction of the essential market of rural labor force. A reference paper prepared for the Ministry of Agriculture, Beijing.

Leading Board of Sichuan Province for the Development of the Poor Areas. 1988. The collections of the governmental documents concerning the performance of the public work schemes of Sichuan. Sichuan.

Lei, Xilu, and Li Renbao. 1980. *Research reports on rural economic development in western regions of China.* Beijing: Planning Publishing House of China.

Li, Changan. 1991. A speech at the National Working Conference for Poverty Alleviation in Minority Nationality Areas, 9 April.

Liaison Office of the Research Center for Rural Development under the State Council, ed. 1984. *Explorations on economic development strategies in border areas.* A collection of research reports. Beijing.

Linqu County Government. 1991. *Strengthening construction of mountainous areas to accelerate steps of poverty eradication (a review on experience).* Linqu.

Liu, Yunjiu, and Qiu Fangjie. 1993. Chances, challenges, and measures. *Development and Getting Rich* 6.

Liu, Zhongli. 1993. The implementation of the 1992 State Budget and the draft State Budget for 1993. Report, 16 March, Beijing.

Local History Compiling Committee of Linqu County. 1991. *Local chronicles of Linqu.* Jinan: Shandong People's Publishing House.

Ministry of Agriculture and the State Council Leading Group for the Economic Development of Poor Regions. 1987. A joint circular on supporting poor regions in the development of the use of plastic films in hybrid maize production. Beijing.

Ministry of Civil Affairs, the Ministry of Finance, the State Economic Commission, and the Agricultural Bank of China. 1985. A report asking for instructions on supporting poor rural households by developing production. 18 March.

Ministry of Finance, People's Bank of China, and Ministry of Commerce. 1985. Financial regulations concerning the public works projects by using grain, cotton, and cloth stock. Beijing: People's Republic of China.

_____. 1987. Financial regulations concerning the public work projects by using middle- and low-grade industrial goods. Beijing: People's Republic of China.

Ministry of Health Care. 1976. The standard for drinking water. Beijing: People's Republic of China.

Ministry of Hydroelectricity. 1980. The report about the problem of the shortage in rural drinking water. Beijing: People's Republic of China.

_____. 1984. The regulations about rural drinking water supply. Beijing: People's Republic of China.

Ministry of Transport. 1990. The transport of China during the reform, 1978-1988. Beijing: People's Republic of China.

Ningxia Autonomous Region of Hui Nationality, Agricultural Construction Committee. 1992. Introduction on poverty alleviation programs in Ningxia. A working report. Yinchuan.

Ningxia Traffic Bureau. 1992. Introduction on transportation programs for poverty alleviation. A working report. Yinchuan.

Office of the Leading Group for Economic Development of Poor Areas Under the State Council. 1989a. A collection of documents on economic development in poor regions. Beijing: The People's Publishing House.

_____. 1989b. The outline of the development in poor areas. Beijing: People's Republic of China.

Office of the State Council Leading Group for Economic Development of Poor Regions. 1991. The main situation in the work of poverty alleviation and development in China. Working report. Beijing.

Pindyck, R. S., and D. L. Rubinfield. 1992. *Econometric models and economic forecasts*. U.S.A.: McGraw-Hill, Inc.

Planning Commission of Wangcang County. 1991. *The general plan of relief works in Wangcang County during the 8th Five-Year Plan.*

Policy Division of the Ministry of Agriculture. 1992. Memorandum of Chinese rural policy research, 225. Beijing: Reform Publishing House.

Provincial Government of Guizhou. 1989. The reform and opening to the outside of Guizhou in the period of 1978-1988. Guiyang.

Ranis, G., and S. Kuo. 1978. Growth and the family distribution of income by factor components. *Quarterly Journal of Economics* (February).

Ravallion, M. 1990. *Reaching the poor through rural public employment*. World Bank Discussion Paper 94. Washington, D.C.: World Bank.

RCRD (State Council Research Center for Rural Development). 1984. The development studies on the western regions of China. Beijing: People's Republic of China.

Regional Division under the State Planning Commission and the Sichuan Provincial Office for Yigong-Daizhen. 1991. *A guidance for the work of Yigong-Daizhen*. Beijing: Publishing House of the Science and Technology Papers.

Research Group for Economic Development of Poor Areas. 1989. From balanced growth to development pole. *Forum on Economic Development* 10, Beijing.

_____. 1990. An analysis on extrication from poverty by qualification of the poor farmers: A qualitative analysis on economic behaviours of rural households in low income areas. *Forum on Economic Development* 11, Beijing.

Research Office of Shandong Provincial Committee of the Chinese Communist Party. 1986. *Status of Shandong Province*. Jinan: Shandong People's Publishing House.

Rural Survey Team of the State Statistical Bureau. 1989. On the measurement of the Chinese poor areas. A research report. Beijing: People's Republic of China.

_____. 1990. The distribution of rural poor, poor households, and poor areas in China. A research report. Beijing.

Shandong Provincial Planning Commission. 1990. A working report on Yi Gong Dai Zhen projects in Shandong Province. Jinan.

Shandong Provincial Statistical Bureau. 1991. *Statistical yearbook of Shandong*. Beijing: Statistics Publishing House of China.

Sharma, U. 1990. Social welfare programme for women and children in India. *Social Change* 20 (2), New Delhi.

Shi, Zheng. 1985. A discussion on the economic development in the western regions of China. *Development Studies* 4, Beijing.

Sichuan Provincial Office for Yi Gong Dai Zhen Projects. 1989. Documents compiles.

State Council Leading Group for the Development of Poor Areas. 1989. A circular on fixing the areas under plastic film: Maize growing and supporting the poor regions with plastic films and chemical fertilizers. Beijing.

State Planning Commission. 1984. The notification on helping the poor areas to construct roads and water conservancy-irrigation system with grain, cotton, and cloth. Beijing: People's Republic of China.

_____. 1987. The notification on helping the poor areas to construct roads and water conservancy-irrigation systems with middle- and low-grade industrial roads. Beijing: People's Republic of China.

_____. 1988. The report about the performance of the public work projects by using grain, cotton, and cloth stock. Beijing: People's Republic of China.

State Science Commission. 1986. Outline of the report on the inspection of the Dabie Mountain areas. 25 April, Beijing.

State Statistical Bureau. 1982. *Statistical yearbook of China.* Beijing: People's Republic of China.

_____. 1989. *Statistical yearbook of China.* Beijing: People's Republic of China.

_____. 1990. *The yearbook of Chinese population census, 1990.* Beijing.

_____. 1991. *The Chinese yearbook of statistics 1991.* Beijing: Chinese Statistics Publishing House.

State Statistics Bureau, Census Department. 1991. *The yearbook of Chinese population census, 1991.* Beijing.

State Statistics Bureau, Department of Social Statistics of Chinese Countryside, ed. 1989. *The essentials of rural economic statistics of Chinese Counties 1980-1987.* Beijing: Publishing House of Chinese Statistics.

State Statistics Bureau, General Team for Social Economy in Chinese Countryside, ed. 1992. *The essentials of rural economic statistics of Chinese counties 1990.* Beijing: Publishing House of Chinese Statistics.

Statistics Bureau of Ningxia. 1991. *Yearbook of Ningxia statistics.* Beijing: Statistics Publishing House of China.

Statistics Bureau of Sichuan Province. 1992. *Statistical yearbook of Sichuan.* Beijing: Statistics Publishing House of China.

Statistics Bureau of Wangcang County. 1981. *A collection of statistical data of national economy, 1981.*

_____. *1990.* The yearbook of statistics of Wangcang County, 1990.

Teklu, T. 1992. The experience of labor-intensive public works programs in the 1980s: The potential for improving food security in Botswana. International Food Policy Research Institute, Washington, D.C. Mimeo.

Tong Zhong, S. Rozelle, B. Stone, Jiang Dehua, Chen Jiyuan, and Xu Zhi-
    kang. 1994. China's experience with market reform for commercializa-
    tion of agriculture in poor areas. In *Agricultural commercialization,
    economic development, and nutrition*, ed. J. von Braun and E. Kennedy,
    119-140. Baltimore, Md., U.S.A., and London: Johns Hopkins Univer-
    sity Press.
Traffic Bureau of Guizhou Province. 1988. Work instead of relief-
    development transport. Guizhou Province.
_____. 1989. Motor roads and economic development. Guizhou Province.
Traffic Bureau of Puding County. 1990. The report about the performance
    of rural road construction projects. Puding County.
Wang, Xiaoqiang, and Bai Nanfeng. 1987. *The poverty of plenty*. Chengdu:
    Sichuan Publishing House.
Wang, Xinhuai. 1993. The 'Yigong Daizheng' policy of Chinese Govern-
    ment. A paper presented at the International Policy Workshop on Em-
    ployment for Policy Alleviation and Food Security. Airlie House, Va.,
    U.S.A., 11-14 October.
Wangcang County, Family Planning Commission. 1992. Reforms on im-
    plementation of family planning. A working paper.
Wangcang County, Office for Poverty Alleviation. 1990. Profile of the rural
    poor households in Wangcang County. Statistical tables.
Wanmali, S. 1992. *Rural infrastructure, the settlement system, and devel-
    opment of the regional economy in southern India*. Abstract of Re-
    search Report 91. Washington, D.C.: International Food Policy Research
    Institute.
Webb, P. 1992. Food security through employment in the Sahel: Labor-
    intensive program in Niger. International Food Policy Research Institute,
    Washington, D.C. Mimeo.
World Bank. 1990. *World development report 1990*. Oxford: Oxford Uni-
    versity Press.
_____. 1992a. *China: Reform and the role of the plan in the 1990s*.
    Washington, D.C.
_____. 1992b. *China: Strategies for reducing poverty in the 1990s*.
    Washington, D.C.

_____. 1993. *World development report 1993*. Oxford: Oxford University Press.

Xiji County Government. 1991. The work reports on five-year programs of food and cloth security.

_____. 1992. Improving work of cadres on poverty alleviation at township and village level. A work report.

Xiji County Statistics Bureau. 1984. Economic statistics of Xiji County for the year 1984.

_____. 1990. Economic statistics of Xiji County for the year 1989.

Yang, Zhong. 1993. Chinese Government measures in the alleviation of rural poverty and in food securities. A paper presented at the International Policy Workshop on Employment for Policy Alleviation and Food Security. Airlie House, Va., U.S.A., 11-14 October.

Yunjiu, Liu, and Qiu Fangji. 1993. Chances, challenges, and measures. *Development and Getting Rich* 6.

Zhang Xietan. 1988. Discussions on economic reforms of minority areas. In *Economic development forum 3*. Beijing.

Zhang, Yiming. 1991. Agricultural construction of San Xi areas: Successful experience of regional anti-poverty programs. *Economic Development Forum* 2, Beijing.

Zhao, Zhuyan, and Xu Shibin. 1993. Thinkings on the collection of funds inside the health and medical institutions. *Chinese Health Economy* 8.

Zhou, Binbin. 1990. A rethinking on the basic policies of poverty alleviation during the period of the 7th five-year plan. *Economic Development Forum*, 12, Beijing.

_____. 1991. Poverty problems in period of people's communes. *Economic Development Forum* 3. Beijing.

Zhu, Ling. 1990. Effects of public works on economic growth, employment, and social services in poor areas. Economic Research No. 10. Beijing.

_____. 1991. *Rural reform and peasant income in China*. London: The Macmillan Press, Ltd.

_____. 1992. Impact of nonagricultural activities on patterns of rural income distribution. *Economic Research* 3, Beijing.

Zhu, Ling, and Jiang Zhongyi. 1990. Impacts of Yigong-daizhen on poor areas of China. International Food Policy Research Institute, Washington, D.C. Mimeo.

_____. 1994. *Public works and poverty alleviation.* Shanghai: SAN LIAN Bookstore and Shanghai People's Publishing House.

Subject Index

A

advanced technology, 119
Africa, 195
antipoverty policy, 17
antipoverty strategies, 6, 7, 8, 49
arable land, 39, 113, 142

B

basic industries, 29
Beijing, 195, 196, 197, 198, 199, 200, 201, 203
Brazil, 148
Britain, 179, 196

C

capital goods, 123, 160, 161
checks and balances, 154
coastal areas, 168
collectivization, 15
commodities, 45, 129, 142, 154, 155, 158, 166, 182, 190
Communist Party, 14, 31, 163, 195, 200
competition, 168, 170, 178
construction work, 4, 40, 53, 54, 76, 77, 96, 112, 115, 117
consumer goods, 23, 24, 118, 123, 129, 130, 134, 136, 144, 159, 160

consumption, 23, 53, 81, 118, 133, 134, 136, 137, 141, 142, 145, 164, 189, 195
countryside, 35, 76, 134, 172, 173, 174, 176, 177, 178, 185, 192

D

daily necessities, 34, 45, 136, 181
decentralization, 154, 160, 180
defense, 182
division of labor, 99, 145
domestic market, 170
drinking water, 4, 5, 23, 24, 25, 34, 36, 41, 46, 49, 53, 54, 55, 60, 68, 74, 78, 82, 87, 119, 122, 133, 148, 153, 154, 155, 157, 161, 186, 197, 198

E

East Asia, 3
ecological environment, 13, 21, 32, 33, 39, 44, 46, 50, 141, 142
economic development, 10, 14, 15, 19, 21, 27, 31, 131, 168, 177, 186, 197, 198, 199, 200, 202

economic growth, 1, 2, 3, 7, 18, 19, 20, 21, 29, 32, 36, 43, 50, 56, 77, 110, 147, 149, 151, 169, 177, 178, 179, 186, 187, 191, 203

economic reform, 2, 3, 7, 8, 27, 29, 59, 82, 114, 152, 155, 172, 178, 185, 191, 203

economic reforms, 2, 3, 7, 8, 27, 29, 59, 82, 114, 152, 172, 178, 203

education, 5, 13, 18, 21, 47, 49, 83, 85, 94, 95, 96, 130, 145, 150, 156, 171, 172, 173, 174, 176, 177, 178, 180, 182, 189, 191, 196

educational level, 99, 122, 170, 172

employment, 3, 6, 15, 19, 21, 24, 43, 51, 81, 94, 101, 113, 114, 117, 133, 150, 157, 167, 169, 170, 179, 182, 185, 192, 199, 202, 203

entrepreneurs, 155

Europe, 34

F

family farms, 58

family planning, 13, 33, 44, 47, 50, 59, 202

farm production, 33

farmers, 2, 3, 8, 10, 15, 17, 21, 24, 25, 29, 34, 37, 39, 40, 41, 43, 44, 45, 46, 48, 50, 51, 54, 58, 59, 64, 65, 76, 77, 78, 99, 107, 108, 110, 114, 115, 118, 121, 123, 124, 128, 129, 130, 133, 136, 137, 141, 142, 149, 150, 157, 160, 161, 163, 164, 166, 169, 176, 177, 185, 187, 188, 190, 195, 200

fertilizers, 37, 45, 68, 119, 122, 123, 165, 166, 200

financial administration, 154

financial subsidies, 17, 167

Food Consumption, 133

Food Security, 164, 202, 203

food shortages, 43, 50, 110, 133, 136, 145, 154, 164, 167, 187, 190, 191

foodgrain, 8, 9, 15, 20, 23, 33, 34, 35, 39, 42, 43, 44, 45, 46, 48, 64, 164, 165, 166

G

Great Britain, 179

Gross National Product, 29

Guizhou, 4, 12, 186, 199, 202

H

health care, 18, 23, 150, 171, 174, 176, 178

Hebei Province, 4

human resources, 13, 21, 24, 47, 85, 124, 150, 172

Hungary, 34

I

illiteracy, 8, 13, 85, 95, 172, 173
Income Composition, 103
Income Inequalities, 110
India, 71, 96, 117, 200, 202
industrial goods, 23, 198
inflation, 181
infrastructure, 2, 3, 18, 22, 23,
  24, 29, 43, 50, 51, 56, 60, 68,
  71, 77, 94, 110, 114, 117, 118,
  120, 121, 123, 124, 130, 146,
  149, 150, 151, 156, 185, 187,
  189, 190, 195, 202
Inner Mongolia, 12
international organizations, 40
investment, 3, 4, 18, 19, 21, 22,
  23, 24, 53, 54, 65, 78, 85, 96,
  100, 103, 117, 124, 128, 129,
  130, 148, 149, 150, 151, 152,
  153, 154, 156, 157, 158, 159,
  160, 161, 167, 170, 172, 173,
  176, 177, 180, 188, 189, 190,
  191
irrigation, 32, 34, 37, 39, 46, 49,
  58, 97, 122, 141, 142, 200,
  201

J

Japan, 29

K

Korea, 29, 148

L

labor force, 24, 29, 39, 40, 52,
  64, 71, 77, 83, 85, 87, 95, 100,
  101, 115, 122, 148, 151, 152,
  153, 167, 197
labor mobility, 108, 119, 131
Laiyuan County, 4
land ownership, 2, 15, 113, 122
land reform, 2
Latin America, 3
life expectancy, 8, 13, 172
life quality, 191
living standard, 8, 16, 148
local economy, 17, 43, 50
local government, 10, 17, 24, 25,
  31, 46, 51, 52, 54, 55, 56, 146,
  148, 154, 155, 156, 157, 160,
  164, 165, 173, 181, 186, 187,
  190

M

mainland, 12
Malaysia, 196
market mechanism, 58, 60, 160,
  191
market mechanisms, 3, 58, 60,
  160, 191
market regulation, 22
marketization, 6, 158, 163, 164,
  166, 168, 169, 171, 177, 179,
  183, 191
marriage, 47
medical services, 122, 174, 176,
  178, 179, 196

migration, 2, 130, 169, 170
minority nationalities, 13, 14, 15,
    20

N

Ningxia Hui Minority
    Autonomous Region, 32
Nonagricultural Employment,
    167
nonfarming sectors, 31, 119
nonpoor regions, 17, 18, 156,
    158, 191
Nutrition, 133, 136, 137, 197

P

peasant households, 4, 103, 107,
    108, 109, 113, 114, 117, 152
People's Bank of China, 198
People's Congress, 9, 159, 161,
    163
personnel, 49, 52, 168, 172, 197
planned economy, 16, 22, 58, 65,
    151, 154, 157, 158, 160, 161,
    162, 163, 168, 169, 190
political stability, 10
poor population, 1, 2, 3, 7, 8, 9,
    10, 11, 14, 21, 22, 34, 36, 37,
    39, 178, 179, 187
population growth, 13, 42, 44,
    47, 51, 171
poverty alleviation, 3, 7, 8, 9, 10,
    16, 17, 18, 19, 20, 21, 22, 24,
    25, 27, 32, 39, 41, 44, 47, 48,
    50, 59, 113, 131, 136, 147,

148, 150, 152, 155, 156, 157,
    158, 166, 169, 178, 179, 180,
    182, 185, 186, 188, 189, 191,
    192, 196, 197, 199, 203, 204
Poverty Eradication, 179
Poverty line, 8
preferences, 76, 117, 118
public investments, 17, 149, 155,
    159, 191
Public roads, 25
public works, 3, 20, 27, 31, 36,
    41, 45, 51, 55, 56, 76, 77, 78,
    82, 117, 150, 153, 158, 162,
    186, 188, 195, 198, 201, 203

R

road construction, 4, 25, 32, 60,
    74, 100, 128, 186, 202
rural areas, 2, 12, 22, 129, 134,
    172
rural economy, 18, 58, 185
rural population, 2, 9, 13, 14, 18,
    31, 37, 41, 43, 113, 185

S

Shandong Province, 27, 29, 31,
    36, 37, 95, 123, 144, 200
Shanghai, 41, 204
Sichuan Province, 5, 34, 35, 36,
    44, 94, 123, 161, 187, 197,
    201
social services, 3, 20, 24, 42, 43,
    49, 65, 68, 71, 82, 94, 119,
    121, 130, 133, 148, 149, 152,

172, 177, 178, 180, 182, 187, 203

soil erosion, 13, 33, 39, 46

South China, 95, 141

sovereignty, 158

steel, 160

subsidies, 17, 20, 43, 78, 164, 166, 167, 169, 181, 182

surplus labor, 24, 41, 43, 101, 148, 169

T

Taiwan, 29

taxation, 17, 157, 181

Tibet, 12

transportation, 2, 4, 5, 13, 19, 20, 25, 27, 29, 31, 34, 35, 36, 45, 52, 53, 65, 107, 112, 128, 136, 154, 156, 157, 161, 164, 199

V

Village Communities, 57, 71

W

wages, 24, 76, 81, 108, 109, 114, 119, 130, 150, 157, 182, 189, 192

Wangcang County, 4, 5, 36, 44, 45, 46, 47, 48, 49, 51, 55, 60, 74, 94, 107, 109, 123, 138, 141, 142, 145, 186, 199, 201, 202

water conservancy, 18, 31, 32, 37, 39, 43, 52, 78, 146, 156, 161, 190, 200, 201

water conservation, 21, 23, 25

water supply, 4, 5, 23, 24, 25, 36, 41, 53, 60, 64, 68, 78, 82, 100, 122, 151, 161, 186, 197, 198

Western China, 12

western regions, 12, 13, 14, 197, 199, 200

World Bank, 167, 169, 172, 174, 178, 180, 199, 202

X

Xiji County, 4, 5, 41, 42, 43, 44, 50, 74, 95, 108, 123, 141, 142, 145, 186, 203